Managing Corporate Liquidity

Lance Moir

The Association of Corporate Treasurers

The Association of Corporate Treasurers is a professional body, formed in May 1979, to encourage and promote the study and practice of finance and treasury management, and to educate and train those involved in this field. The Association currently has 1800 Members, 600 Associates and more than 1500 students. It is the only UK body which concentrates and sets professional examinations exclusively on the subject of finance and treasury management. The Association is an independent body, governed by a Council of Members whose work is supported by a number of active voluntary committees.

Managing Corporate Liquidity

Lance Moir

Glenlake Publishing Company, Ltd.
Chicago • London • New Delhi

AMACOM
American Management Association
New York • Atlanta • Boston • Chicago • Kansas City • San Francisco • Washington, D.C.
Brussels • Mexico City • Tokyo • Toronto

This book is available at a special
discount when ordered in bulk quantities.
For information, contact Special Sales Department,
AMACOM, an imprint of AMA Publications, a division of
American Management Association,
1601 Broadway, New York, NY 10019.

This publication is designed to provide accurate and authoritative
Information in regard to the subject matter covered. It is sold
with the understanding that the publisher is not engaged in
rendering legal, accounting, or other professional service. If
legal advice or other expert assistance is required, the services of
a competent professional person should be sought.

Printing number

10 9 8 7 6 5 4 3 2 1

Contents

Contents

Preface

This book has been written in order to describe how the basic management of liquidity operates in companies – both domestic and multinational. In particular, it attempts to set some of the basic decisions in liquidity management (how much do I deposit, for how long and at what rate) in the overall business context.

However, it does not claim to be a complete study of liquidity. In particular, the details of money transmission, debtor and creditor control and international trade finance are excluded, while there is only a rudimentary examination of short term deposit and borrowing instruments.

It is written not only for the student of treasury management, but also for non-financial executives who need to know what liquidity management is all about. It should also be useful for the small business person who will meet the concepts of liquidity management every day.

Liquidity is only part of treasury management, and so certain problems which arise from a lack of liquidity naturally lead directly on to the ability to raise debt and other issues. Funding management and corporate finance and these developments are deliberately beyond the scope of this book. Nevertheless, surrounding events have to be considered when applying any liquidity management technique, but I hope that this book places liquidity management in the general business context and will be suitable both for the treasury specialist and general business person alike.

Since the first edition was published in 1992, the use of liquidity instruments and, in particular, interest rate hedging has developed considerably. This has been a period when sterling left the ERM and the markets learned the true meaning of volatility and when a number of large companies throughout the world have lost money using derivatives. The second edition of this book looks at interest rate hedging in much more detail and also sets out more control mechanisms which have been developed by the ACT and other bodies.

Liquidity management now fits more closely with currency management and other aspects of money management. This book, however, tries to pull out the essential elements of liquidity management which remains at the beginning of all treasury management – without available cash, the business will fail.

I am grateful for the continuing support of all the staff at the Association of Corporate Treasurers.

This edition is dedicated to the memory of my parents, Renee and James Moir.

Lance Moir
June 1997

1

What is liquidity and how does it arise?

- The definition of liquidity
- The broad objectives of liquidity management
- How liquidity impacts on a business

What is liquidity?

The liquidity of an organisation is the ability to make payments as they fall due. Perhaps more important are the consequences of illiquidity which are likely to lead to a business ceasing to trade.

A company may be highly profitable in an accounting sense, but this is of no use if there is no cash to pay employees and suppliers and no cash to make further investments. Conversely, a company which is making large accounting losses may be generating substantial cash (e.g. early in the 1980s Courtaulds made substantial accounting losses, yet generated millions of pounds before repaying loans and paying dividends). This may be the result of writing off assets or by creating accounting provisions as well as high levels of depreciation.

Although the availability of liquidity to a company is the prime objective, that liquidity also requires active management in order to benefit the company in a financial sense, but also to avoid and minimise risk.

The scope of liquidity management usually extends to the management and control of:

- cash flow and cash flow forecasting;
- investments and borrowings of up to 1 year;
- availability of borrowing facilities;
- short term interest rate management.

It will also cover detailed applications including money transmission, and debtor and creditor management.

How does liquidity arise?

In order to manage effectively a company's liquidity, it is important to understand how it arises and the uses that it is put to. In particular, there is a need to understand the dynamics of the business, particularly in so far as these affect the cash flow. For example, as sales grow, a business must assess how much extra cash is consumed by working capital (or, less commonly, for some businesses such as large food retailers, how much cash is generated).

As part of the normal business cycle, liquidity arises:

1 By generating profits in cash terms; that is, through selling goods for cash in excess of that required to produce them. This will be made up of a number of cash flows, both in and out:
   (a) cash sales;
   (b) receipts from debtors;
   (c) payments to creditors;
   (d) operating costs;
   (e) capital invested;
   (f) dividend and interest payments.

2

Naturally it follows that if the business is either growing or inefficient, then liquidity is consumed rather than generated. Inefficiency also includes increasing stock levels greater than needed to meet sales. Stock positions, however, arise as a combination of the purchase of raw materials and slow cash sales rather than as cash movement in themselves.

2 By selling for cash assets that are no longer necessary.
3 By raising funds (either debt or equity) in excess of the amount needed for investment by the company at that time. This might typically happen where a company has a planned expansion programme and decides that it would be prudent to raise the necessary finance in advance (e.g. pharmaceutical development or oil exploration).

Liquidity is consumed:

1 By making new investments in fixed assets, or acquiring businesses.
2 By increasing working capital in order to expand sales or improve margins.
3 By making losses in excess of the depreciation (and other non-cash) charge.

These are the factors that affect liquidity over a long term business cycle, but on a day-to-day basis, more significant factors are likely to be receipts and major payments to suppliers or for payroll. For many small businesses, it is items such as these that really represent liquidity.

It is important to note the emphasis on cash in the above lists. The amount of cash available can be measured unambiguously, whereas other accounting treatments can be more subjective. The amount of cash used in working capital is particularly important and in situations of illiquidity it is often working capital that can be squeezed first to generate liquidity, where other assets will take longer to realise.

For many businesses, the emphasis in liquidity management is associated with *working capital management* – that is, ensuring that payments from debtors are received swiftly, stocks minimised and payments to creditors delayed until the latest commercially sensible date. However, the key feature of liquidity management is the *availability* of liquidity, therefore for businesses which are not trading at their limit, this is often the borrowing facilities available, typically overdrafts for small businesses (but also committed borrowing facilities for larger companies) or investments that are liquid, such as bank certificates of deposit or quoted securities.

How does liquidity management fit into treasury policy?

Every business should have a clear set of treasury policies that establish the board's attitude towards the various treasury activities, such as the level of risk to be adopted, the level of gearing (and therefore the amount of debt to be raised) and who is authorised to deal on the company's behalf. Within these policies, there should be sections setting out the policy towards liquidity management, in particular covering:

- cash management;
- short term investment management;
- short term interest rate management;
- money transmission management.

These policies cannot stand independent of the total treasury activity – for example, short term interest rate management should fit with the overall risk profile. Money transmission will depend upon the group's attitude to centralisation – do all international payments net through a centre or are they managed locally?

The objectives of cash management policy

The policy on cash management for a large group should comprise at least the following:

1 A brief description of the origins of short term cash and funding positions around the company.
2 The objectives of the policy, for example to provide adequate and cost effective banking services for the company and its subsidiaries by:
   (a) minimising the level of funds in subsidiaries while ensuring the provision of short term financing for day-to-day working capital requirements;
   (b) maximising the income from short term surpluses held in bank accounts, and minimising the cost of short term deficits, through active management of bank account balances;
   (c) ensuring that, where possible, the most efficient and cost effective banking practices are observed.
3 A standard for the bank account configurations across the company. This should define the optimum number of banks to be used and the cash management facilities that should be provided, interfacing with group-wide systems where appropriate, including netting and pooling (see Chapter 4).
4 The standards for local treasury dealing facilities, where required, including overdrafts, deposits and foreign exchange dealing lines, including a company-wide standard bank mandate.
5 Policy on the use of parent company guarantees, letters of comfort and other support agreements.

6 Where not specified elsewhere, a list of authorised counterparties, with associated at-risk limits. These will link into the bank relationship management policy.

7 Where not specified elsewhere, a reference table of authority limits for opening bank accounts and establishing local banking relationships.

What are the objectives of short term investment management?

The sheer importance of continuing liquidity to a business has led to a very strong trend towards centralisation of cash and general treasury management within groups. The small business always has to concentrate on cash flow, and this is also true in the largest multinational group. Other policies are discussed later in the book. However, it is appropriate to set out the objectives of short term investment management here as the philosophy is important to understand up-front.

The prime objectives of short term investment management are:

1 *Liquidity*. The business must be able to meet its liabilities as they fall due.

2 *Safety*. Investments should not be exposed to the risk of an unacceptable loss in capital value, and borrowing facilities should continue to be available when needed (i.e. there is no point in having borrowing facilities available if the prospective lender is about to fail).

3 *Profitability*. Only once it is certain that the first two objectives can be met, can the question of return be considered. There will always be a trade-off between risk and reward, but there must also be a clear view of how much risk the business is prepared to accept and whether the reward is enough to compensate.

Once these objectives have been satisfied, flexibility may also enter the picture. Whereas the availability of liquidity should always be considered for the range of likely business events, there may also be alternatives available in the selection of deposit instruments or interest periods. All other things being equal, the more flexible alternative will always be more desirable.

Liquidity in different industries

While the ultimate objective of ensuring that there is enough cash to pay the bills is the same across all businesses, the nature of the industry will change the way in which it is operated. Clearly, the amount of equity and debt in any given company should reflect the needs of the business and no amount of good liquidity management will be able to compensate for a basic deficiency in the capital structure.

First, suppose that we are running a market stall selling fruit and vegetables. Each day, we will sell for cash and because the product will rot if not sold, we are unlikely to have any significant stock. Equally, we will buy our goods for sale each day, probably from a wholesaler. The ideal position here would be to try to obtain some credit from the wholesaler, but this may only be possible if we are able to offer perhaps a guarantee or when reliable trading has been established. Here, liquidity is very much a day-to-day matter, particularly if any additional staff are employed who need paying on a regular basis.

Suppose, however, that the business does not sell for cash, but against invoice perhaps 60 days away. In addition to any capital costs in setting up the business, there will need to be liquidity available to meet running costs, including purchase of

7

raw materials (if they are paid for in less than 60 days plus the time they are being converted into the end product). This might come from an overdraft facility, from factoring the debtors or from surplus cash from shareholders' funds.

Alternatively, if the business in which we are involved is a company purely researching into pharmaceuticals, with no products foreseeable for some years, then the business will not get very far unless it has enough capital in the form of cash to last for some years. In this case, liquidity becomes a matter of conserving cash and using the strength of high levels of cash to negotiate longer periods for credit taken. Then, there is an opportunity to manage interest income by selecting different periods in which to deposit.

But if we look at more complex groups of businesses, there is a distinct need to understand the cash generation cycle in detail. The larger capital elements such as capital expenditure, new equity or the payment of tax and dividends are readily identifiable, but the cash flows in the working capital cycle need closer examination. The working capital cash cycle is the timing difference between the purchase of raw materials and receipt of cash from their sale after processing. In addition, further costs involved need to be examined. Different businesses will be affected in different ways. Supermarket chains, for example, may have a negative cash cycle as they often pay for goods well after they have sold to the public. If, however, the business is a food company supplying a major supermarket, then a decision by the supermarket to take (say) 3 days' more credit could have an impact of millions of pounds on the suppliers.

A normal working cash cycle might be depicted as in Figure 1.1.

Let us consider the broad liquidity issues of three different businesses: food manufacturing, fashion retailing and heavy engineering.

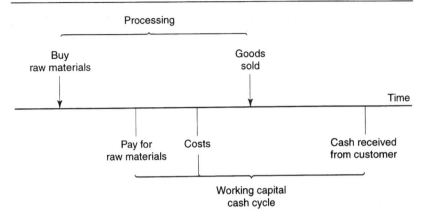

1.1 A normal working cash cycle.

A food manufacturer

Once the purchase of capital equipment has been established, the working capital cycle will be critical. The timing of the purchase of raw materials may be dictated by availability of supply, whereas the sale of finished products may be dictated by an entirely different market, possibly in different countries. The importance of credit periods taken by customers has already been noted and systems will need to be in place to identify changes.

A fashion retailer

As opposed to a food retailer, a fashion retailer will again be dependent on the working capital cycle. Goods will be ordered and paid for in advance of sale (possibly before they are even in the shops if they are imported). Therefore, there will be the cash consumed both by advance payment and by stockholding. Cash will then be received when the goods are sold. Unlike a food manufacturer, therefore, the individual elements of payments to suppliers and receipts from sales will need to be monitored separately (in a business where sales and purchases are more closely connected, it might be possible to monitor the net position). Additionally, the seasonality of this type of business means that each month will need to be considered individually.

A heavy engineering company

Clearly the initial capital investment in plant and machinery is going to be the most significant item in this type of company. After that, the liquidity management once more centres on control of working capital and operating costs. Accounting systems will be based upon depreciating capital equipment and may show large losses that disguise the cash movements. Raw materials will be bought on credit, but the manufacturing process may mean that large amounts of cash are tied up in work-in-progress (and this figure will increase with very large items such as aircraft engines). Finished stock may then also be held for long periods and, although no cash may actually be moving at this point, liquidity may continue to be consumed if further products continue to be manufactured. Finally, sales will probably be made on credit and control of the period extended will be needed. In this instance, the amount tied up in working capital may not only be significant, but unlike the retailer, it is also illiquid. This means that working capital in this type of business needs to be financed from longer term sources of finance.

So in this way (and in many others) different industries have different ways of managing liquidity.

2

Forecasting liquidity

- The importance of the cash forecast
- Different methods of preparing the cash forecast
- Problems that arise in practice

The importance of the cash forecast

As has been explained in Chapter 1, the availability of cash to meet liabilities as they fall due is central to the continued existence of businesses. In order to be certain about the availability of cash and how to manage it, there is a need to prepare cash forecasts on a regular basis. One way to ensure liquidity is to maintain large cash balances or arrange necessary borrowing facilities, which may be expensive, but neither of these approaches will result in optimal profitability. Therefore, reliable cash forecasts are essential in order to minimise idle cash balances and reduce loan costs and hence improve results.

Cash forecasts are normally prepared on different time-scales and there are different methods associated with these timescales. The degree of accuracy involved will also vary with the approach used. Cash forecasts are normally prepared on the following timescales:

1 The forecast for the next day. This will need to be accurate. Its principal use is to calculate the borrowing or depositing need for that day. For businesses that are trading at the limit of their facilities, it will also be used to see who can be paid! Indeed, businesses that get into financial difficulty often have failed to maintain reliable cash forecasting – because they were too busy selling or manufacturing.

2 The very short term forecast, which looks at likely cash flow over the next few days; this includes cheques drawn and about to be received through the banking system, as well as cash receipts and other known payments. This also ought to be fairly accurate.

3 The short to medium term forecast, looking about 6 months forward. This gives the general shape of the cash flow and allows various alternative funding and investment decisions to be made.

4 The long term forecast, looking at perhaps 4 or 5 years (or even longer in major capital-intensive industries). This is, in effect, the cash element of the corporate plan and will form the basis of the funding strategy.

The shorter horizon forecasts (i.e. up to the next few days/ weeks) will be based on 'cleared funds', that is those that are available for use and for interest purposes. Longer term forecasts can work off broader forecasts associated with sales and profits.

The way that cash forecasts are designed will depend on the structure of the company and the nature of its business. However, any cash forecast will be prepared in order to show the following:

- the amount of cash surplus or requirement;
- when the cash surplus or requirement will arise;
- how long the cash surplus or requirement will last;
- how the cash will eventually be used or generated;
- in what currency the cash will be available or needed.

Example: Jackets Limited

Consider the retail company Jackets Limited (Table 2.1). This is a company which has been expanding fast, but has high and growing profit margins. To the outside world, it seems as if it is a good credit risk to its suppliers and is a successful business. Yet, the amount of trade credit has expanded.

Table 2.1 Jackets Limited: financial information

	Year			
	X1	*X2*	*X3*	*X4*
Sales (£000)	586	921	2204	3937
Profit before tax (£000)	21	107	406	616
Gross margin (%)	39.9	43.3	47.3	49.7
Net margin (%)	3.6	11.6	18.4	15.6
Earnings per share (p)	0.28	1.02	4.15	6.22
Balance sheet (£000)				
Fixed assets	89	178	453	1027
Stock	77	196	484	971
Debtors	10	31	49	129
Cash	1	1	1	1
Bank overdraft	(31)	(41)	(49)	(225)
Trade creditors	(43)	(103)	(211)	(519)
Other creditors	(36)	(100)	(158)	(210)
Taxation	(8)	(39)	(192)	(352)
Long term creditors	(6)	(4)	(6)	(95)
Provisions	(8)	(15)	(18)	(16)
Net assets	45	104	353	711
Creditors/sales × 360	26	40	34	47
Stock/sales × 360	47	77	79	89
Debt/net assets × 100	69	39	14	32

Ostensibly, the ratio of debt to equity is within reasonable limits, yet the company has available borrowing facilities of only £500 000 which are on a demand basis and fall due for review 3 months after the year-end. Indeed when we look more closely it can be seen that the suppliers have been financing the business.

When we add the information that the accounts are prepared at the year-end, which represents a low point in cash terms ahead of seasonal stock requirements, we can see how little use formal accounts are in the liquidity management of a business as these do not tell the whole picture. In a business such as Jackets, in the early part of the year it will have to buy a large proportion of its stock before it has earned any profits and when it may also want to spend capital expenditure on development. The borrowing needs could easily exceed £1 million.

But if we extend the forecast by a further year and assume some physical expansion, we can see that the company cannot continue to grow without a significant injection of capital before the consideration of the seasonal aspect. This demonstrates the importance of attention to cash flow forecasts in the management of business (Table 2.2). (Note: these cash flows have been summarised to show the total picture.)

This forecast has been prepared on an annual basis. If we were to look more closely at the next 3 months, we would see that the seasonality of the business leads to growing stock during that period. Unless trade credit can be extended to an extreme level, the company will not be able to continue to trade because of lack of raw materials. So what looked like a long term problem may become a short term crisis which may give the owners of the business few options. In fact what seemed like a need to raise either equity or long term debt to finance expansion becomes a crisis of how to continue to trade over the coming months. The eventual reality of this situation

14

Table 2.2 Jackets Limited: cash flow

	X4	X5 (forecast)[a]
Profit	616	700
Add: Non-cash	129	175
	745	875
Increase in stock	(487)	(600)
Increase in debtors	(80)	(100)
Increase in creditors	360	450
Tax paid	(85)	(175)
Operating cash flow	453	450
Capital expenditure	(717)	(750)
Dividends	(15)	(15)
Disposal of assets	14	0
Other	(4)	0
Net cash flow	(269)	(335)

[a] The forecast for year X5 assumes further expansion at the current rate and also assumes the continued willingness of suppliers to advance credit.

was a need to find nearly £1 million to satisfy pressing creditors which was only resolved by a quick sale of the business. Thus the lack of clear planning arising from timely cash forecasts reduced the options available to the business.

It is clear that the absence of timely cash flow forecasts obstructed any planning and reduced the options available, whereas the preparation of such forecasts would have allowed the management to take well planned decisions. It would also have given them the confidence to persuade bankers and investors to support the company. Most importantly, it would have allowed them options which might not have been available in a crisis.

15

Uses of cash forecasts

Before considering the techniques of preparing cash forecasts, it is useful to review their end uses. If these are considered at an early stage, then the particular form of any report prepared can be designed in advance. It will also allow the necessary degree of accuracy and frequency of the forecast to be taken into account:

1 Short term:
   (a) advance warning of liquidity problems;
   (b) availability of funds to make payments;
   (c) level of funds available to deposit;
   (d) shortfall in funds to be borrowed;
   (e) confirmation of short term trading forecasts.
2 Medium term:
   (a) funding and depositing profile;
   (b) exposure to interest rate and currency risk.
3 Long term:
   (a) funding strategy;
   (b) major investment decisions;
   (c) ability to meet corporate objectives and dividend policy;
   (d) exposure to interest rate and currency risk.

The basic format can be prepared at business unit/individual company level and then consolidated for group purposes at the required level of detail. For example, in decentralised groups it may be enough to consolidate the flows of individual companies and then add group movements. In other situations it may be more appropriate to separate out capital expenditure and other cash flows which do not arise from day-to-day trading. These alternatives are discussed in greater detail later in this chapter.

Preparation of the cash forecast

There are two main methods of preparing cash forecasts – the receipts and payments method and the sources and uses method. They tend to be applicable to different situations and are complementary rather than direct alternatives.

In both cases, prior to consolidation on a group basis, each forecast should be prepared by major currency and major legal entity. Note the emphasis on major – there is no need to spend so much time preparing forecasts that there is no time to act upon them. As much effort as is required to provide all meaningful information to a suitable degree of materiality should be spent, bearing in mind the cost of preparation, but no more.

The receipts and payments method

At its most basic, this involves listing all the receipts which are expected to be received during the forecast period and deducting the payments expected to be made. This net flow is then added to the opening position to give a forecast closing position.

If you were to attempt to prepare a personal cash forecast for the coming month, this might be done by starting with your opening bank balance, adding salary and other receipts and then deducting mortgage payments or rent, cost of food and travel, etc to give a closing bank balance for the end of the month. Preparation of a company's cash forecast takes this same basic principle into a business context.

A basic format might look like that given in Table 2.3. This basic forecast would be prepared at business-unit level. Therefore, not all the categories would be appropriate (such as divi-

Table 2.3 Basic format of receipts and payments method

	Period 1	Period 2
Opening balance		
Receipts		
Sales in cash		
Receipts from debtors		
Sale of assets in cash		
Tax receipts		
Other receipts		
Inter-company receipts		
Total receipts		
Payments		
Suppliers in cash		
Wages		
Rent		
Utilities		
Other costs		
Capital expenditure		
Dividends		
Tax		
Other		
Inter-company payments		
Total payments		
Net movement		
Closing balance		

dends) and it may be desirable to introduce others. It would be necessary to define first the period(s) to be forecast and the level of detail required (e.g. hundreds, thousands, etc. of relevant currency).

Points to note:

- All figures are cash, so sales does not mean all sales, just those made in cash. But receipts in cash from sales made in a previous period are included.
- Similarly, all costs and payments to suppliers are not included, only those made in cash, but payments to creditors in the current period are included.
- It is often useful to try to list inter-company payments separately, as group analysis will be particularly interested in external cash flow.
- There is no reference to stock.

This forecast is likely to be prepared by a cashier's department and so may not include payments under the control of more senior management. Therefore, controls will be needed to ensure that all known major payments are covered by the forecast at some level.

While normal trading payments are generally well controlled and therefore forecast, one-off payments such as major asset sales and items of capital expenditure are often forgotten – usually because 'everyone knew about it'. Therefore, for critical forecasts such as a daily one for the next few days, the end user of the forecast will have to consider carefully whether all major payments are included.

In a group, the individual forecasts will be consolidated to produce a combined trading position. The group treasury department will then need to add the treasury transactions to produce the net figure available for investment or to be borrowed over the period. Such a format might be as that given in Table 2.4. This format does not differ in concept from that

Table 2.4 Format of receipts and payments method for a group

	Period 1	*Period 2*
Opening position		
Receipts		
Trading flow		
Maturing investments		
Interest income		
Foreign exchange		
New borrowings		
Other		
Total receipts		
Payments		
New investments		
Interest payments		
Foreign exchange		
Dividends		
Tax		
Maturing borrowings		
Other		
Total payments		
Net movement		
Closing position		

used by the trading business, but concentrates on the payments made by or to a central treasury department. These payments should tie in to the diary system which should be maintained by any treasury department. Care will be needed to ensure that any receipts or payments included in the trading flows are not duplicated in the treasury forecasts.

Particular notes are:

- As with the trading forecasts, care needs to be exercised that all payments are cash payments, e.g. interest.
- Individual forecasts should be prepared by currency, therefore foreign exchange means cash flows in that currency. This may mean that there is a corresponding flow in a different currency cash forecast.
- 'Other' may include items like option premia, FRA settlements (see Chapter 8).
- Tax and dividends may be necessary given the increasing use of separate companies for treasury functions, but again care should be exercised to ensure the matching flow is reflected if payments are intra-group.
- Care should be exercised to ensure that there is clear treatment of loan roll-overs. In particular, it is often better to show these as a repayment and fresh borrowing. This will allow a clearer decision to be made on the period of the new borrowing.

Limitations of the receipts and payments method

The receipts and payments method of forecasting is very good for short periods. It can often be tied in to known cheque runs or receipts from sales already made. However, the technique of forecasting the cash position from individual items means that these items are considered in isolation from each other, therefore a particular bias in one figure can lead to a nonsense over a longer forecast. For example, if a conservative approach is taken to future sales (and this is often very sensible), then a

21

forecast read on this basis over a year may lead to a ridiculously high stock position. Equally, the consideration of cost items individually may result in a ridiculously high or low profit result. This is because this method looks at cash in a different way from the main accounting systems, precisely by not considering accounting-driven terms such as profit or stock levels.

Therefore, over longer periods it is often more useful to use the source and application method of forecasting cash. The principal use of this method is that it ties in to normal financial control systems and can be used to set clearer objectives for operational management.

Example: Robins

Robins PLC is a company which manufactures computerised manufacturing systems. It has accepted a contract from Modern Manufacturing Systems PLC (MMS) to supply an integrated manufacturing system to a new factory which MMS is building. The contract represents a substantial share of Robins' business for the current year.

Base rates are currently 12% (1 September 199X) and Robins finances itself from overdrafts, except for a fully drawn term facility at 13% pa of £2 million which expires on 31 December 199X + 1.

The price for the contract has been agreed with MMS at £2.0 million and MMS will pay 50% of the contract price on 30 November 199X and the balance on 28 February 199X + 1.

The contract begins on 1 September 199X and runs for 6 months. In order to fulfil the contract Robins purchased components on 1 September for £1.6 million. This purchase was for cash and will be followed by four successive monthly payments of £50000 by Robins to cover installation costs for the system. The first of these payments takes place on 1 November 199X. MMS has agreed to reimburse Robins in full in addition for installation costs 1 month after they are incurred.

Robins has been experiencing difficulties in its working capital management over the last 2 years; its overdraft has risen sharply and as at 1 September 199X stood at £4 million. Its bank requires it to fall to £3.5 million by 31 March 199X + 1 and not to increase in the meantime. Robins' treasurer has proposed the following as the means of financing the working capital requirements of the MMS contract:

1 Robins will increase the credit taken from suppliers for the normal business from its usual 2 months to 3 months, beginning with certain invoices which would have been due for settlement at the end of each of the 3 months from 30 September and to attempt to maintain this lag thereafter. Each month's invoices which are to be delayed are worth £800 000. The cost of this additional credit is the loss of discounts worth £40 000 per month starting with October's discounts.

2 Robins will reduce its orders for stocks by £100 000 per month for the first 3 months of the contract. Destocking will take the form of reduced orders for raw materials and components placed with suppliers. Stocks are planned to be returned to their established levels by an order for £300 000 for raw materials and components placed on 31 December 199X.

3 Robins will factor trade debtors worth £2.1 million on 1 September. The factor will take a fee of 5% of the debts factored and will pay 90% of the value of the debtors to Robins on 1 September and the remaining 5% on 1 October. The debts factored represent 3 months' sales at £700 000 per month and would normally have been paid in equal instalments on 1 October, 1 November and 1 December.

It is to be assumed that, apart from the MMS contract, Robins would be able to work within its existing facilities.

Review of this action and the resultant cash forecast

The monthly cash flows resulting from the MMS contract and the treasurer's proposed actions based on the information given above can be forecast using the receipts and payments method.

The technique is to identify the differences that arise from the contract. In particular, because factoring has been used to accelerate payments, the normal cash flow has to be deducted later on (see Table 2.5).

Thus it can be seen that even with these actions, the overdraft limit will still not meet the bank's requirements and there may be some loss of business goodwill given the delay to creditors. A more certain form of finance will need to be found. The cash forecast above also excludes the impact of interest charges which would be required for a more detailed review.

The sources and uses method

Whereas the starting-point of the receipts and payments method is sales, the sources and uses method starts with profit. Therefore, a considerable number of assumptions have already been made and should already have been scrutinised by the responsible operational management and at the appropriate level by the financial controller. This issue is considered in greater detail in Chapter 3.

Before describing the format and technique of preparing this forecast, it is important to stress that this is not exactly the same as the cash flow statements under UK or US GAAP. Although accounting standards are evolving, the format suggested here could also be used to control the cash within the business. The format in Table 2.6 concentrates on cash flows and aims to be almost brutal in identifying how the business is being funded.

Table 2.5 Cash flow forecast for MMS contract (£000)

	1.9.9X	1.10.9X	1.11.9X	1.12.9X	1.1.9X + 1	1.2.9X + 1	1.3.9X + 1
Contract price				1000			1000
Components	(1600)						
Installation costs			(50)	(50)	(50)	(50)	
Reimbursement				50	50	50	50
Reduction in stock			100	100	100		
Restocking	(300)						
Receipt from factor	1890	105					
Lost cash flow from debtors		(700)	(700)	(700)			
Delays in payments to creditors		800					
Lost discount			(40)	(40)	(40)	(40)	(40)
Net cash flow	290 / (4000)	205	(690)	360	60	(40)	710
Overdraft	(3710)	(3505)	(4195)	(3835)	(3775)	(3815)	(3105)
Analysis of cash flow							
Contract	400						
Factor	(105)						
Creditors	600						
	895						

Cash flow assumptions:

1 Contract price: Dates given (30 Nov = 1 Dec; 28 Feb = 1 March).

2 Components: Initial purchase of £1.6 million given at 1.9.9X.

3 Installation: Given as commencing 1.11.9X (with 1 month stagger for reimbursements).

4 Creditors: Delay invoices worth £800000 starting at 30.9.9X (= 1.10.9X); 1 month stagger; loss of discount of £40000 associated with payments of creditors with 1 month's delay.

25

Table 2.6 Format for sources and uses method

	Period 1	Period 2
+ Profit before tax		
+ Depreciation		
− Associates' profits		
+/− Other non-cash items		
− Profit on asset disposals		
− Increase/(decrease) in stock		
− Increase/(decrease) in debtors		
− Tax paid		
+ Increase/(decrease) in creditors		
+/− Other short term movements		
Trading cash flow		
+ Asset sales		
+ Dividend receipts		
+/− Other long term/non-recurring receipts		
+ Receipts from associates		
− Capital expenditure		
− Dividend payments		
− New investment in associates		
Net movement		

26

Each business will design a layout more suited to its own needs and which may also give a better fit to the management accounts.

Note that there is a deliberate split between short term and long term items. The purpose of this is to identify how much cash the business is generating or consuming from day-to-day activities. Many external lenders and investors in group situations will expect the trading cash flow to be able to fund new capital expenditure and dividend payments. If the trading cash flow is negative then this may point to an unsustainable business or one which is consuming too much cash in working capital (alternatively, this may be part of a deliberate business strategy for a growing business). This format will allow the treasurer to make pertinent comments to his or her colleagues about the cash flow of the business.

As with the receipts and payments method, the basic forecast can be prepared at business-unit level, therefore it may be useful to introduce lines for inter-company payments.

Different businesses will have different concepts of profit. It will be useful to try to express the true underlying level of profit by excluding non-recurring items such as profit on property sales and extraordinary and exceptional items. These frequently include non-cash elements which obviously do not form part of a cash forecast. For cash elements, it is better to show these separately in the bottom half of the forecast.

When calculating the movements in the components of working capital, careful separation of any unusual elements such as a debtor due an uncompleted property sale will allow a better understanding of what is actually going on as well as helping to calculate the business cash flow.

For all other elements, the need is to concentrate on the cash which is actually going to flow in the period under consideration. Virtually all of these items should be generated by a normal management accounts package.

27

Many of the points for special attention described in the preparation of a receipts and payments forecast still apply here – in particular the risk that large or irregular items are forgotten just because they do not form part of routine control.

Once each business unit's forecast has been prepared and these have been consolidated on a group basis, if necessary, then there is the need to add the following lines to take account of major capital flows:

- – debt repayments;
- – new deposits;
- + maturing deposits;
- + new debt receipts;
- + fresh equity receipts.

Notice that interest payments and receipts have not been mentioned explicitly. This is because their treatment depends on the particular style of internal management reporting.

If it is usual to show profit post-interest then it is necessary to ensure that there have been correct adjustments in debtors and creditors. A safer treatment would be to show profit before both interest and tax and then show cash interest payments and receipts in the same manner as tax.

Example: Conglomerate

Conglomerate Inc is the holding company of a group of companies. The operating portion of the group in the US consists of three wholly owned subsidiaries, Sellit, Makeit and Developit. Sellit is a chain of supermarkets with national coverage; Makeit manufactures building materials; and Developit is a property development company specializing in major office developments.

In Table 2.7 are extracts from the balance sheets of the three group companies. For each of the companies data are given for the financial year just ended and from the budgeted balance sheets for the coming year. Table 2.8 shows data derived from the budgeted profit and loss accounts of the three companies for the coming year. Turnover in the year ended 31 August 1997 was as follows: Sellit $2536 million, Makeit $3392 million and Developit $370 million. The capital budgets of the three companies for the year are summarised in Table 2.9.

The budgeted financial information has been prepared on assumptions about the operations of the three companies and the market conditions in which they are expected to operate.

Table 2.7   Selected balance sheet data for group companies, year ended 31 August 1997 and budgeted for the year to 31 August 1998 ($ million)

	Sellit		Makeit		Developit	
	Year ended 31.8.97	Budget to 31.8.98	Year ended 31.8.97	Budget to 31.8.98	Year ended 31.8.97	Budget to 31.8.98
Fixed assets	1416	1617	1205	1265	982	989
Current assets						
Stock	179	192	392	499	108	173
Debtors	49	39	500	535	25	55
Cash	27	79	89	72	2	5
Creditors of less than 1 year						
Overdrafts	59	2	116	116	6	9
Trade	286	332	131	146	30	30
Taxation	45	69	105	43	9	2
Other (excluding provisions)	53	100	17	24	4	4
Provisions	40	50	22	30	1	1

Table 2.8 Budgeted profit and loss account data for the year to 31 August 1998 ($ million)

	Sellit	Makeit	Developit
Turnover	2984	3571	533
Profit after interest and tax	185	250	80
Depreciation	69	117	30
Provisions for future redundancy expenses	13	5	–
Profit on disposal of fixed assets	5	20	13
Interest costs charged to profit and loss	39	85	30
Interest costs capitalised	31	–	15
Interest received	41	16	5
Taxation charged for the year	40	30	5

Table 2.9 Summary capital budgets of US operating companies ($ million)

	Sellit	Makeit	Developit
Capital expenditure	385	257	55
Disposals of fixed assets (at net book value)	115	80	18

Sellit has been assumed to continue to increase its market share in a very competitive retailing market while continuing to reduce unit costs and increase its net profit margins. Developit's profits depend crucially upon the sale of a large office development. Negotiations for its sale are at an advanced stage but have been stalled and there is doubt about whether the sale will be completed.

Sellit's operating cash flows arise regularly through the year. Its capital expenditure plans for the coming year are part of a programme of new store development begun some years ago and which is expected to continue for several more years. Makeit's capital expenditure programme for the coming year is expected to be at its height during autumn/winter 1997/98. Developit's expected cash flows are dominated by the planned sale of the major office development referred to above. If the sale goes ahead it will occur towards the end of the company's accounting year.

Review of the resultant cash forecasts

The annual cash flows of Sellit, Makeit and Developit for the year ending 31 August 1998 can be forecast using the sources and uses method (see Table 2.10).

This layout allows the main sensitivities to be observed and also shows that Makeit is highly cash generative before capital expenditure.

Using the two methods in combination

In the same way that the receipts and payments method is inappropriate for longer term forecasts, the sources and uses method would be unwieldy for short term forecasts and would also not allow an adequate level of control.

Depending upon the pressures within the business, the level of control and accuracy will vary. So, for example, a business experiencing severe liquidity problems would require very precise daily forecasts for perhaps the next 4 weeks, all prepared on a receipts and payments method. These would be followed by weekly forecasts for the following 2 months, again prepared by the same method. Then, a sources and uses method might be used for the following 3 months. If the liquidity problems

Table 2.10 Cash flow forecasts for the three companies for the year ending 31 August 1998 ($ million)

	Sellit	Makeit	Developit
Profit	185	250	80
+ Depreciation	69	117	30
Provisions	13	5	–
Capitalised interest	(31)	–	(15)
	236	372	95
Less profit on disposal of fixed assets	(5)	(20)	(13)
Adjusted cash flow	231	352	82
Stocks	(13)	(107)	(65)
Debtors	10	(35)	(30)
Creditors	46	15	–
Tax paid	(16)	(92)	(12)
Operating cash flow	258	133	(25)
Capital expenditure (less interest capitalised)	(354)	(257)	(40)
Disposal of fixed assets	120	100	31
Other creditors	47	7	–
Provisions	(3)	3	–
	68	(14)	(34)
Increase in overdraft	(57)	–	3
Decrease in cash	(52)	17	(3)
Therefore, reduction in other borrowings	(41)	3	(34)
Borrowings at 31.8.97	213	421	550
Budgeted other debt at 31.8.98	254	418	584
Fixed asset reconciliation			
Opening FA	1416	1205	982
+ Capital expenditure	385	257	55
– Depreciation	(69)	(117)	(30)
– Book value of assets sold	(115)	(80)	(18)
Closing FA	1617	1265	989

Table 2.10   (*Continued*)

	Sellit	Makeit	Developit
Tax payment			
Opening balance	45	105	9
Charge to P&L	40	30	5
Closing balance	(69)	(43)	(2)
Therefore, cash payment	16	92	12

were severe, going further could be an unnecessary diversion of management time.

However, in normal circumstances, a typical profile might be:

1 Receipts and payments:
   (a) daily for the next 3–5 days;
   (b) weekly for the following 3–12 weeks.
2 Then sources and uses:
   (a) monthly for the remainder of the year;
   (b) annually for the following 2–4 years.

Thus there would be a gradual build-up of a cash profile over the next 5 years.

For months 4–6 there could be a blending of the methods, by paying particular attention to the underlying assumptions for working capital and by taking special care over large items.

When considering the forecasts for the next few months, however they have been prepared, it will be important to identify the peak borrowing requirement within a month. If forecasts are prepared on a month-end basis and the peak cash outflow occurs mid-month, a false sense of security might occur, especially for companies near to the limit of their borrowing facilities.

A summary of the relative advantages of the two types of forecast is:

Receipts and payments

- It uses the skill and experience of the treasurer, who normally develops a considerable 'feel' for the way the cash moves.
- It is simple in concept.
- It relies on items that are easily known and forecast for relatively short periods, say for the horizon of the existing sales ledger balances; this is in many cases around 3 months.
- It is suited to computer spreadsheets.

Sources and uses

- It integrates with the general financial control and reporting process. A receipts and payments based forecast would not be capable of identifying absurdities such as future negative inventory.
- It signals the implications of forecast cash movements. An escalating stock position or mounting losses call for management action, yet they are not visible from the receipts and payments forecast.
- It produces a forecast balance sheet, which is particularly useful to management.
- It tends to be more accurate in the long term. The treasurer's forecast can only extrapolate existing or past, normal or seasonal trends and patterns of wages and trade receipts and payments.

Problems in groups

While the theory of forecasting cash extends to groups by consolidating individual subsidiaries or divisions, there are a number of practical points which may cause problems.

Even though the cash forecast may have been prepared by reliable colleagues in subsidiaries or other group functions, the treasurer should still examine the forecasts submitted for commercial sense and internal consistency. Errors can and do occur – what is important is the availability of reliable figures rather than apportioning blame.

Cash-book or cleared balance?

A cleared balance is the amount of cash in the bank which has passed through the clearing process (see Chapter 4) and is available for use to receive interest or reduce interest charges. For short term purposes, this is the figure that the treasurer should use for funding and investment decisions. The cash-book figure is the accountant's figure of cash and will include cheques banked and exclude cheques written. However, many of these cheques will not have completed the clearing cycle (indeed, some cheques may still be in the post to the suppliers) and so the bank's view of cash available (or overdrawn) is not the same as the accountant's view. In large groups, the difference may represent millions of pounds.

It is important, therefore, to issue clear instructions on how the forecast is to be prepared. In practice, it will be preferable to prepare forecasts for the next few days (and certainly for the close of the current day) on a cleared basis. Individual business units can provide details of cheques issued and make reasoned assumptions on the number of working days taken for cheques to clear through the system. Similarly, agreements will have been reached with banks on the clearing cycle for payments lodged and these can be factored into the forecast.

Longer term forecasts can be supplied on a cash-book basis, particularly as this will be consistent with other business forecasts. The treasurer can then make a necessary group adjustment for interest forecasts.

In businesses with severe liquidity problems, minds will be particularly focused on the cleared position, but an eye will need to be kept on large cheques being specially presented.

Different assumptions

It usually goes without saying that clear instructions should be given for preparation of all business forecasts in well run groups. However, cash forecasts are prepared at different times and more frequently than profit forecasts. Therefore, the treasurer will need to review all forecasts for consistency. These include standard assumptions about interest and exchange rates, but most importantly about the timing of payments.

Intra-group payments are a particular problem, where disputes between subsidiaries can often mean that the paying unit will not forecast for political reasons. This does not help the treasurer and only clear and rigorous rules will solve the problem. It is always necessary to check that all intra-group payments match.

For particularly large items, such as the sale of a building, the cleared versus cash-book problem becomes particularly acute. The only practical solution is for the treasurer to ask for detailed information and then to act on it independently. Over time, a wider understanding will assist, but the risk of different assumptions will never be totally removed.

Who prepares the forecast?

In spite of clear instructions, the treasurer does not have ultimate control of the preparation of the forecast in the subsidiary. Often a great deal of education may need to take place before forecasts are submitted to the required standard on a consistent basis. A particular risk arises from the use of the sources and uses method. One of the great advantages of this method is that it is supposed to tie in with the other business forecasts. This will be negated if the cash forecast is calculated by one person and submitted independently from the other forecasts. It is helpful, therefore, to insist that longer term cash forecasts are submitted with profit forecasts, thus forcing the subsidiary finance director to focus on internal consistency. If this does not happen, there could be the embarrassing position of a substantial difference between the treasurer's view of the future cash position of the group and that of the financial controller!

Informal arrangements and group politics

The treasurer has a different function in a group from that of the controller or divisional finance director. A prime need for the treasurer is to understand exactly what will happen to the cash position on any given day – others may be more concerned with setting and meeting targets. Thus, it may not be uncommon for targets to be set and forecasts produced which the division knows cannot be met precisely. Thus, payments may actually be 2 or 3 days late, but it would be politically unacceptable to submit this forecast to the centre (or even to the divisional chief executive officer (CEO)). Alternatively, a particular division may knowingly set optimistic targets for its own reasons.

The treasurer has to try to obtain all relevant information to establish the cash position as well as to determine the most likely outcome. Therefore, it may not be unusual for the treasurer to establish an informal network of contacts with the divisions to ensure that there is a reliable flow of information. This network is likely to be the very people who are submitting the forecast. Naturally, the role of the treasurer extends to getting out into the divisions in order to understand their business, both to manage the liquidity of the group and also to represent the group effectively to the financial community. The operation of such an informal arrangement will be an art in itself and will bring the treasurer's interpersonal skills to the fore.

Obtaining the opening position and other data

As with all forecasts, it is essential to know the starting position. The most accurate method of obtaining the opening position is to ask the bank. This may be done either by telephone or via an on-line balance reporting service (see Chapter 4). It is likely to be supplied on a cleared basis, but will also provide useful information on payments due to clear during the current day. It is most unlikely that this will be the same as was forecast the previous day. A brief variance analysis will need to be carried out to ensure a better forecast for the day.

For longer term forecasts, prepared on a cash-book basis, a reconciliation between cash and cleared will allow a better understanding of the forecast, although the cash-book opening position will be the figure that ultimately will be used.

Bank reporting systems will also be able to provide details of payments and receipts clearing over the next two days. Other major items such as payroll, pensions, dividend payments and taxation will be provided by the relevant departments to be compiled into a daily forecast.

Currencies and multinational groups

The introduction of a number of currencies essentially complicates matters only to the extent of needing to prepare a forecast for each currency. The treasurer will then need to take particular care to ensure that intra-group trade has been forecast consistently *by currency*. Then the various internal foreign exchange deals will need to be entered to provide a net position by currency. Armed with the forecast, the treasurer may then decide to convert currencies in surplus to those in deficit so as to reduce net interest charges. It is clear that this level of complexity can only be managed by suitably integrated computer programmes – otherwise the time taken on calculations will exceed available daylight hours in which to take decisions.

Conclusion

Cash forecasts are important in the financial management of a business and are central to many decisions. However, the time spent on them and the detail of their preparation will be dictated by the size and financial condition of the organisation. The techniques set out in this chapter can be used by businesses of all sizes, but the frequency of preparing and reviewing forecasts will depend upon the circumstances.

3

The management of uncertainty

- How to begin to take decisions when real life does not turn out as originally forecast

Preparation of a cash forecast is all well and good, but it is not an end in itself – cash forecasts have to be used. In Chapter 2, the main uses of cash forecasts were described. However, simply because a cash forecast has been prepared does not mean that, for example, the level of borrowings forecast would be the appropriate level of facilities to be arranged. Forecasts need interpretation.

More importantly, it would be startling if reality always matched the forecast position. Life may not turn out the way that has been expected, items may have been missed out, there may be forecasting bias or simply errors. Therefore, each forecast will need to be considered carefully from a number of viewpoints in order to decide what to do.

In a practical sense the main use of an overnight forecast would be to ensure that the balance on the current account is maintained as close to zero as possible, but slightly overdrawn. This is because credit balances on current accounts rarely earn interest and it would be better to place funds on deposit. Consider the following situation:

Company X has forecast that cash balances in the current account will be £250000 in credit – current account debit interest is 8%, current account credit interest is 2.5% and an overnight money market deposit rate is 6%.

	Interest	*Yield*
If the £250000 is left on the current account:		
Interest received = 250000 × 2.5% × 1/365	£17.12	2.5%
If the current account is left £250000 overdrawn:		
Deposit £500000 overnight		
Interest = 500000 × 6% × 1/365	£82.19	
Less overdraft costs		
Interest = 250000 × 8% × 1/365	(£54.79)	
Net interest	£27.40	4.0%

So, because of the steep differential in interest rates it is almost always better to leave a current account in debit where possible and invest overnight. Thus, it can be seen that a primary use of an overnight cash forecast is to estimate the smallest amount that would definitely leave a current account in debit. In the scenario here, the additional £250000 overdrawn above and beyond the forecast amount would allow for any errors or unanticipated receipts.

This approach assumes that it is possible to leave an account in debit. There are two main situations where this would not be possible:

1 *It is illegal.* In some jurisdictions current accounts must be in credit. Therefore, mechanisms should be found to feed the account from other deposits.
2 *There are no borrowing facilities.* This would be true for a business in financial difficulty or where there is no track record.

In both these situations, the objective would be to leave the account as close to zero as possible, but in credit.

Therefore, in assessing any particular forecast there is a need to establish the possible range of outcomes. These different outcomes may arise either from error or bias or alternatively from uncertainty.

Checking against past forecasts

As with all forecasts, it is often instructive to compare reality with previous forecasts. This has a number of benefits:

1 It looks for bias by the person preparing the forecast. The main use of a cash forecast is to establish the borrowing or investment requirements of the business and, as such, it is the absolute amount required or available that is important. So, if a particular individual takes a cautious view on sales, this may be compounded in a group situation if the treasurer takes the same view. If the existence of bias can be established, then the output of the forecast may be interpreted.
2 It helps to identify structural changes in the business. It may be, for example, that cash has followed a particular seasonal pattern in the past and that this has continued in recent forecasts. Any changes in a fast-moving business tend to be identified most quickly by changes in cash positions.
3 It will help to avoid illiquidity by looking for longer term errors and over-optimism in past forecasts. This type of analysis should also be carried out for associated accounting forecasts. Crucially, though, this focuses on the cash position.

A typical variance analysis could be represented graphically (Figure 3.1).

Seasonal PLC has prepared forecasts over a number of periods (Table 3.1). Thus, in period 0, the forecast for two periods ahead was (84), this was revised to (85) in period 1 and actually

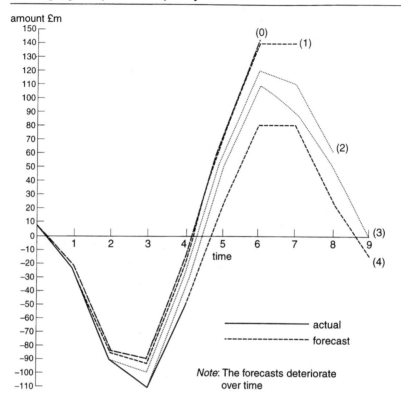

amount £m

3.1 A typical variance analysis.

turned out to be (90). In this case forecasts have been consistently over-optimistic, representing a belief that sales will eventually recover. We will return to this company in Chapter 9.

This type of analysis should clearly show any of the trends
described above. Any forecast should be expected to vary from
the actual result within a realistic margin. This may represent
a percentage of sales or receipts. Naturally any significant variance should be investigated. If bias within a division is the

Table 3.1   Seasonal PLC: cash forecasts (£m)

Date	\textit{Forecasts prepared in period}					
	0	*1*	*2*	*3*	*4*	*5*
0	8A					
1	(22)	(24)A				
2	(84)	(85)	(90)A			
3	(90)	(93)	(100)	(110)A		
4	(15)	(20)	(25)	(40)	(50)A	
5	73	75	60	50	20	
6	143	140	120	110	80	
7		140	110	90	80	
8			60	50	25	
9				0	(15)	

A = actual.

cause, it may be more politic in the first instance to recognise the bias and to compensate for it. In the long term, however, such a bias will need to be removed, and control procedures instated to try to avoid biases and errors in the future.

Once a particular team of people has been preparing forecasts for some time, familiarity will lead to an intuitive understanding of the likely outcome and the action required. However, consistent and high quality reporting must be maintained to avoid complacency.

Trends or detail

A question that frequently arises is whether to look at detailed variances or just to consider the trends. In some ways this is related to the timescales involved.

Frequently, variances to forecast are explained by very cogent reasoning, such as this sale did not arise or that happened late. However, if trends are looked at, these may show a consistent pattern – the management issues which generally arise from such a realisation are beyond the scope of this book – but the treasurer will be able to recognise the consequences and act accordingly.

In the short term, however, detailed examination is important as this will show more detailed errors in reasoning. Also, it might point out any compensating issues that could arise – such as receipt from a delayed sale. Alternatively, a cash forecast might only have been achieved by delaying payments to creditors. These will have to be met at some stage.

The condition of the business will also direct the emphasis. Clearly, a business in a liquidity crisis will need to consider the detail. A more secure business will be able to concentrate on trends. However, the detailed examination will need to be prepared by someone, but possibly more as part of a control process.

How much liquidity is needed?

Even with the benefit of analysis of past forecasts, life is still unlikely to turn out the way expected. This will not be a fault of the forecasting techniques, but because business assumptions vary from reality.

So, what could be different?

- changes in the economic environment;
- cancellation of a major contract;
- success in an unexpected contract;

46

- an unexpected acquisition is made;
- an unexpected disposal is made;
- forecasting errors in business assumptions;
- the board changes its mind.

And, on a smaller scale:

- increase in bad debts;
- pressure from creditors to accelerate payments;
- lack of stock control leading to increased cash.

The central issue is how to use the cash forecast despite the effect of all these variables.

Sensitivity analysis

A practical approach is to attempt a sensitivity analysis, particularly for medium term forecasts. Items such as sales and purchases can only be estimates and therefore an assessment of, say, a 5% variance, particularly on timing, could be undertaken. The actual percentage to be used will be determined by experience of previous forecasting errors.

The key requirement of liquidity management is to ensure that there is enough cash to meet liabilities as they fall due. Therefore, for all relevant time horizons, the treasurer will need to look critically at the cash forecast and consider how reality might vary in order to establish how liquidity requirements could be met. These might be achieved by maintaining large cash balances or by arranging the necessary level of borrowing facilities or by a mixture of the two. There will be a trade-off of cost against the returns the business can generate. On a short timescale, consider the following situation.

Company A

The cash forecast for Company A shows that the bank position on a cleared basis tonight will be £500 000 in credit and that the company has an overdraft facility of £250 000. It is not in the interest of the business to leave credit balances on a current account not earning interest. Therefore, the normal procedure would be to deposit perhaps £600 000 to give an overdrawn balance of £100 000. However, if past analysis shows that there could be errors of as much as £200 000 in cash forecasts, then this would leave Company A exposed to a breach of its overdraft facility with all the attendant consequences. This is a far greater treasury sin than leaving a credit balance not earning interest.

Therefore, in this instance, a lower deposit of £500 000 would be placed (assuming no other major variables) and the risk would be run of a credit balance of £200 000 (arising from an error of £200 000). Finally, assuming that this business has a reasonable credit standing, a higher overdraft facility should be negotiated. Additionally, it would be worth investing time to discover the cause of the forecasting errors. The scale of the error also needs to be considered – £200 000 may be a lot for a small business, but quite acceptable for a large corporation with sizeable daily cash flows.

Medium term liquidity

For medium and longer term issues, the procedure becomes more complex. The overriding need is to ensure that liquidity will be available when required. There are sources of liquidity other than accessible bank balances; these include:

- investments with a ready market, such as bank certificates of deposit;

- undrawn committed borrowing facilities;
- debtors that may be factored;
- assets with a liquid market.

The specific features of these instruments and markets will be explained in Chapter 6, but what is important for the purposes of this chapter is that their potential availability is recognised. Consider the two simple examples below.

Company B

Company B has $10 million available to deposit for 6 months; however, there is a 50% chance that $5 million will be required for an acquisition in 3 months' time. Interest rates currently favour longer deposit periods.

The specific questions of managing the interest rate problem will be considered in Chapters 5 and 7, but for the purposes of liquidity, the likely need for cash is significant. If further borrowing facilities are not available, then there are a number of options that need to be considered:

1 Deposit $5 million for 6 months and the other $5 million for 3 months and see what life is like then; *or*
2 Invest $10 million in a liquid investment for 6 months, recognising that there may be a capital loss in 3 months if it has to be sold; *or*
3 Invest the $10 million in an illiquid investment for 6 months (which is likely to offer a greater yield than the liquid investment) and ensure that there are available borrowing facilities should the acquisition take place.

Company C

Company C has prepared a cash forecast for the next year which shows that it will only just manage with its available borrowing facilities. The treasurer also believes that there is a risk that sales will begin to turn down. In short, the business risk is high.

The problem here is more general than just selecting an interest period and it would appear that the usual option of negotiating sufficient backstop facilities is not possible. In this instance, there are a number of good business practices that should be implemented to avoid illiquidity:

- frequent forecasts to recognise problems early;
- review the management of working capital;
- prepare to sell certain assets ahead of problems;
- review the potential to factor debtors;
- attempt to reduce stocks;
- attempt to obtain additional trade credit without risking supplier goodwill;
- consider raising equity.

Naturally, real life is going to be more complicated than these examples, both because there will be other issues to be considered and because decisions are seldom this clear-cut. However, there are general principles to be applied in the management of uncertainty. The most important of these is the ability to recognise what might happen and develop strategies to deal with the possible as well as the probable.

The more complex issues of managing uncertainty and liquidity will be re-examined in Chapter 9, while the intervening chapters will look at interest rate management, the use of bank systems and the various markets involved.

4

Money transmission and bank services

- How a banker–customer relationship could be arranged
- Money transmission and electronic banking products
- Organising bank accounts for groups

The banking system is critical to the efficient management of liquidity for all businesses. In addition to the borrowing and depositing services described in Chapter 6 and the hedging products described in Chapter 8, the day-to-day operation of bank accounts and money transmission are essential to the smooth running of a business. In this chapter, we shall look at some of the money transmission and other products that banks offer and that impact on liquidity management.

Managing your banker

First, it is helpful to look at how the banker–customer relationship could operate. There have been many complaints over the past few years about how banks have treated their customers, particularly small businesses. On the other hand, many banks have complained about a trend to transaction, rather than relationship banking by large companies. Transaction banking involves taking each item of business to whoever offers the keenest price, while relationship banking involves a certain amount of give and take on the final element of pricing, in return for consistent service.

In approaching its banker, the business needs to know what its requirements are going to be. It also needs to have decided what its ethic of operation is going to be – relationship or just driven by price. Banks are businesses themselves and need to make a return as well as ensure that bad debts do not arise; however, they are also sensitive to competition on price which might drive away good business. As much as any business would want to ensure the continuing supply at the right quality of an essential raw material and would, therefore, recognise short term price-cutting, then so it should regard its bank as a supplier – of money and related products. Banks have come to offer some products at an effective loss, for example loans to large corporations at fine margins, in order to secure attractive other business, such as foreign exchange and money transmission.

The first stage for the business, of whatever size, is to gain the confidence of its banker, especially if borrowing is going to be involved. Banks make an assessment of the character of the management of a business a very substantial part of any credit judgement. This will often be best achieved by being able to make a clear presentation about the business – what it does and what is anticipated for the future. There should also be a clear explanation of who does what in the management team. Banks are just as interested in the non-financial management as in the more direct contacts.

If borrowing is to be sought, then there should be a clear financial presentation available. This should not just concentrate on profit and loss and balance sheet – important though these are. There will need to be a clear cash flow forecast, possibly in the form shown in Chapter 2. There should be a monthly projection for the following few months, followed by quarterly or yearly projections for the next few years. (Large and profitable businesses may not be required to go through this detailed presentation, as a track record will have been established.) This should demonstrate the ability to repay or refinance borrowings. The projections should show how the loan is to be serviced and repaid. The prospective borrower will also need to be ready to discuss the sensitivities of the business. The bank will want to satisfy itself that the cash flow and the profit projections are consistent with each other – so there will be no point in trying to dress up the figures as a good banker should be able to see what is going on.

The trust and understanding that should be established at this stage will allow a more understanding approach to be taken at any time when there are difficulties, and may also result in more beneficial charges in the light of a consistent business relationship. There are a number of intangible benefits that result from a secure understanding with one's banker. These include:

- The banker will be more prepared to spend time understanding your business problems.
- The bank will be able to identify products that are suitable for the business.
- The banker is more likely to push credit applications to his or her superiors and with more personal commitment.
- Errors (which will inevitably occur) can be sorted out quickly.
- The general level of service should be better.

Of course, these are natural human reactions when anyone takes the time to understand another person, but if banks are approached on the basis of business partners rather than adversaries, then there is more chance of making good progress.

Bank products for money transmission and bank account management

The products described below generally need customising to the particular circumstances. In order to make them most effective, there will have to be a detailed understanding between the appropriate clerical staff in the bank and their opposite numbers in the company.

Money transmission

The business of moving money around, for whatever reason, is a significant issue for business. As companies trade internationally, the logistics become complicated and the cost and amounts involved mean that the potential for loss increases. Money transmission is at the heart of modern banking and banks have invested in systems to manage the process efficiently. Companies can often benefit significantly by devoting time to organising carefully the process of paying and receiving funds. If there is a significant volume involved, putting this business out to tender can result in lower costs, as well as different ideas from different banks on how it can be organised. However, banks frequently find this type of business attractive as it involves income without a lending risk, therefore it should normally be offered for tender to those domestic banks that provide the full range of money transmission services. Equally, for those companies with limited borrowing facilities, it is often helpful to couple the granting of the tender for money transmission with the requirement to provide an appropriate level of borrowing facilities. Bad planning would be to withdraw the money transmission business from one bank, for it only to withdraw a lending facility without a replacement facility in place.

However, no amount of hard negotiation will compensate for poor administration within a company. In particular, the cost of interest for many businesses means that all receipts should be paid into the bank as soon as possible. Many businesses incur significant hidden costs because cheques have to be kept in some form of administration department for reconciliation before they are paid in. This represents a large hidden cost, as well as exposing the business to higher bad debts due to bouncing cheques or to customers changing their minds.

Money transmission issues are different in each country and the techniques for minimising costs and optimising interest will differ. Some countries, such as the United Kingdom, benefit from a centralised clearing system. Others such as the United States are organised on a regional basis. In general, the approach will be the same:

- pay the lowest costs;
- reduce administration;
- automate reconciliation;
- achieve the fastest possible 'value' for interest purposes.

There will need to be a trade-off between the processing costs and the interest costs of delay and indeed banks will structure this into their charges such that costs may be lower or, indeed, non-existent if there is a delay before funds are transferred. For some smaller businesses, obtaining faster value will be more important than the cost. For others a simple evaluation will need to be undertaken.

In order to calculate the break-even of a remittance at which incurring an extra cost to reduce float time is worthwhile, the relative costs and benefits must be compared.

The benefit is calculated as the number of days' float saved (d), multiplied by the marginal rate of interest saved (i), multiplied by the remittance amount (B). The additional cost of speeding up receipt is assumed to be C. The break-even point is when these are equal, i.e.

$$C = B \times \frac{d}{360} \times \frac{i}{100}$$ (note: use 365 for sterling instead of 360)

or, looked at another way, the break-even amount for a cost of C is:

$$B = C \times \frac{360}{d} \times \frac{100}{i}$$

So, if interest rates are 10% pa and the extra cost of an electronic transfer is £15 in order to gain 3 days' interest, then it is worth switching for all amounts greater than

$$\frac{15 \times 36500}{10 \times 3}, \text{i.e. } £18\,250.$$

Methods of money transmission

Methods of transmitting money fall into three broad categories:

1 Cash in the form of notes and coin.
2 Paper based – cheques and some credit card transactions.
3 Electronic – such as wire payments or BACS.

Cash

Most businesses only require cash facilities for petty cash purposes, which is not frequently a significant amount. However, for retailers and others dealing directly with the public, there is often a need to deposit substantial amounts of cash, as well as draw out cash in different denominations of note and coin. (It should be noted that smaller banks, and, in the United Kingdom, building societies and the Post Office, are substantial users of cash in the form of notes and coin.)

Although cash does not have the bad debt possibilities of cheques, it does have substantial costs of collection in the form of insurance, security and bank charges. These can make it more expensive to collect than cheques or credit cards. Companies will negotiate charges for the banking of cash with their business customers (it is far from free) and also clearing cycles in the same way as for cheques. Particular care needs to be taken on the terms agreed with the bank for handling cash. The trade-off between the charge for handling cash and the number of days until value is obtained tends to be much more of a trade-off than for cheques, so it is not unusual to receive a higher quote for next-day value and a lower one for 2- or 3-day value.

For larger businesses, competitive quotes can be obtained if the cash can be delivered in bulk to the bank's bullion centre. Each bank has a number of these around its region and the cash is delivered directly by the company's security carrier. The calculation of the most effective frequency for banking cash and the various costs involved is often complicated and frequently warrants the full-time attention of one individual for some weeks to calculate the optimum arrangements.

Cheques

Cheques are familiar as a method of payment, but there are important differences from the personal situation. The most notable of these are charges and the clearance cycle. Banks charge their business customers both for cheques issued and for cheques paid into the business account. These charges are a matter for negotiation and will depend, in particular, on the volume involved. There are often alternatives to automate payments, thus removing the paper involved and providing an opportunity to negotiate lower charges. Banks sometimes charge as a percentage of turnover; however, it is often desirable to have charges based on the number of cheques involved, rather than be charged as a percentage of turnover. If the business grows, this gives greater scope to control costs.

If there are a significant number of cheques paid in (or if the typical value of each cheque is high), then there should be a clear understanding on when good value can be obtained. This represents not only the date at which funds are available for use, but also the date on which the cleared balance is calculated for interest purposes. Most businesses should typically obtain 2- or 3-working day cycles. However, longer value dating may result in lower charges – although this trade-off should be transparent and will be unattractive for many small businesses trading near the limit of their borrowing facilities.

Credit and debit cards

The use of various types of 'plastic' to pay for goods and services, either in person or over the telephone or internet, is now widespread. Fewer retailers now process voucher slips and these are processed as for cheques. Charges will often be calculated as a percentage of value and this will depend upon a mixture of average transaction size, number of vouchers to be processed and the fraud history in the type of business involved.

The increasing use of electronic terminals both to capture transactions and also to obtain credit sanction means that payments for credit cards are received as one direct credit from the credit card acquirer, net of fees negotiated. These fees will again be related as a percentage of the amounts involved and here scale will play an important part to the extent that certain large retailers in the UK are reported to have achieved fees very close to 1%. For charge cards as opposed to credit cards fees are somewhat higher and before accepting such cards, a careful assessment will need to be made of whether additional sales will actually be achieved.

Smart cards with a built-in memory chip are now being developed (although they are already popular in France). Value is stored on the card and transferred to the retailer at the point of sale. In some countries smart cards are being developed as an alternative to cash; in others the emphasis is on security and avoidance of fraud.

Electronic payments

If large sums have to be sent or received (especially internationally), then various forms of electronic payment, e.g. a telegraphic transfer (TT), are worth considering. These are methods where the funds are transferred electronically either with same-day value or 2-day forward value for domestic payments from the paying business account directly to the receiving account. In order for this to occur, there first has to be an agreement between the payer and receiver concerned that payment will be made this way. The payer will often require some inducement to use this method of payment, as a cheque would doubtless be slower and cheaper.

The major forms of electronic payment in the US and the UK are:

- SWIFT (the Society for Worldwide Interbank Financial Tele-communications) for international payments;
- CHAPS (the Clearing House Automated Payments System) for same-day, high value domestic sterling payments (although there is no minimum value for CHAPS payments);
- BACS (the Bankers' Automated Clearing System) for high volume, low value domestic sterling items subject to 2 days' value, e.g. salary and regular supplier payments;
- ACH (Automated Clearing House) for high volume, low value, domestic US dollar payments;
- CHIPS (Clearing House Interbank Payment System) – similar to CHAPS for dollar payments.

Other systems tend to exist in most developed markets.

For companies within the same group, electronic means are the normal form of payment, but for trading partners there will need to be some commercial agreement to use electronic payments. For some industries, this may represent normal terms, for others a separate negotiation may be required.

In order for such payments to be effective, precise instructions will be needed of the bank and account to which the funds are to be transferred. The recipient should also have an arrangement to be notified when funds are received for large amounts so that they can be put to immediate use.

For international funds transfer, the added complication of different currencies means that the instructions have to be particularly clear and also, if accounts are not held in the relevant currency, it must be clear how the funds are to be obtained or applied. A particular risk here is that if no clear currency instructions have been given, then a significant proportion of the total amount will be absorbed in fairly expensive foreign exchange transactions.

In the UK, large businesses may have a CHAPS terminal of their own which is connected via a modem to their clearing bank's own system. If this type of system is to be used there need to be clear and tight controls on access to it. Once payments have been released to the system they cannot be reversed. A particular way of exercising control is to insist that the system is set up so that payments can only be made to certain preset beneficiaries (say, other group companies or particular banks for their own account).

The most common system within the UK for payments that have to be made frequently, say payroll or to regular suppliers, is BACS. Companies supply details of the payments to be made on a preformatted magnetic tape which is then supplied to their bank. Payments need to be supplied a preset period in advance (usually 2 business days) and once they have been released into the system they cannot be cancelled and payment is guaranteed by the payer's bank. The automation of these payments can often result in substantially lower bank charges. The cost of BACS tends to be only a few pence per item whereas TTs cost pounds (overseas it is sometimes a percentage of the value involved without limit – care should be taken to ensure that a limit is in place otherwise simple transfers may cost thousands of pounds).

In addition, BACS can be used for the efficient collection of funds via the use of direct debits. This is common for public utilities and leasing companies, but it can have a wider application for collecting from general commercial customers. However, from the customer's point of view, it may not wish to give the control implied to its supplier. Similar approaches will apply in the US for the use of CHIPS (or Fedwire payments) and ACH.

International trade

In addition to the basic issue of the costs of transferring funds internationally, trading overseas has the added problems of:

- political risk;
- foreign exchange control risk;
- different banking systems;
- different culture;
- time delays.

The credit and political risks are often avoided by a mixture of using confirmed letters of credit, documentary collections and export insurance. Although they are not the instruments that actually transfer funds, these are products that can reduce the risk of default either by retaining title to the goods until payment has been made or assured (in the case of documentary collections) or by transferring the risk to a bank (in the case of letters of credit). However, exporters and importers need to understand how the various facilities operate and that the various risks involved can be removed (if they cannot, then there have to be very good reasons for the transaction involved).

In any event, the additional common features of international trade are the need for absolutely clear instructions in regard to payment (currency, date and bank accounts involved) together with clarity on the documents to be supplied (bills of lading, drafts, etc) if letters of credit or documentary collections are involved. Before agreeing to any particular terms, it is vital to ensure that they will work in *practice*. For example, if payment is to be received in French francs, do you either have a franc account or have you made appropriate arrangements to sell the francs on receipt? If you are selling via a letter of credit, can you actually supply all the documents, *precisely* as they are set out in the terms of the credit?

Organising group bank accounts

The benefits of grouping together the bank accounts for different companies within the same group arise from economies of scale. These are in terms both of bank charges and of overall interest costs. If, say, two companies are under common ownership and one is borrowing and one has surplus funds, then it is clearly beneficial to try to arrange matters so that interest is only charged on the net borrowed position or that the net surplus is invested most efficiently.

Banks will generally agree to charge interest on this basis (subject to certain safeguards described below) and there are two basic methods of arranging the bank accounts. Banks are now also able to provide reports apportioning interest between group companies; an example is given in Table 4.1.

Banks are able to offer cash concentration accounts, where the treasury department of the company instructs the bank to move funds between accounts, either by telephone or electronically; or the movement of funds can be handled automatically on a preset basis. Cash concentration can enable economies of scale by transferring relatively small balances to a master account. Particular approaches are set out below.

Netting or cash pooling

In this instance, each company maintains the balance on its own account and interest is only charged on the net overdrawn position (there tends not to be interest on credit balance – see Chapter 6 in the section on overdrafts). Interest may be charged to one central account or allocated on a basis specified by the company. It is often helpful, both for taxation and for cultural reasons, to arrange affairs so that interest is charged

Table 4.1 National Westminster Bank PLC interest apportionment service. Interest apportionment for the period from 1 April to 30 April. Group name: XYZ PLC Group. IAS Reference: 0013/000 1

Sort code	Account number		Notional net interest	Notional debit interest received	Notional credit interest paid
60 30 06	01497243	Treasury account	0.00	0.00	0.00
60 30 06	01497189	Parent company	1297.71	1573.35	275.64–
01 10 01	86571133	Subsidiary company No 1	475.40–	465.25	939.65–
50 41 29	36486167	Subsidiary company No 2	228.40	345.77	117.37–
		Totals	1050.71	2383.37	1332.66–
		Notional net interest:	1050.71		
		Less group overdraft interest:	634.89–		
		Treasury position:	415.82		

Interest formulae debit rate 2.0000% above base rate.
Base rate from 1 April to 30 April 13.0000%.
Created on 2 May, Time: 0855.

and credited at the same rate to all group companies, with the net effect that the whole group has only been charged on the net position.

The net position is calculated for all group accounts held with a particular branch, irrespective of branch. The central treasury department will hold a central account which is the one that will be used to arrange the desired net position.

Table 4.2 is an example of a netting system. In this example, the treasury department would transfer more than £600 000 from its central account and place it on deposit or use the funds elsewhere, so that net interest would be charged on the (hopefully small) net overdrawn position. In this case, the balances on subsidiaries B and C have been used to offset the costs for A for the group overall.

In addition to the scale economy benefits, there is also the benefit that the individual companies are allowed to continue

Table 4.2 A netting system

	Forecast closing balance (£)	
Subsidiary A account	500 000	Dr
Subsidiary B account	950 000	Cr
Subsidiary C account	150 000	Cr
Net total	600 000	Cr

Table 4.3 Zero-balancing

	Forecast closing balance (£)		Transfer in/(out) (£)
Subsidiary A account	500 000	Dr	500 000
Subsidiary B account	950 000	Cr	(950 000)
Subsidiary C account	150 000	Cr	(150 000)
Net transfer to treasury account			600 000

to operate their own bank accounts, but are relieved of day-to-day treasury management. Therefore, this system works well in decentralised groups where operational management is given a high level of autonomy. It also allows clear control if cash targets have been set company by company.

Zero-balancing

In a netting system, no actual funds move between accounts, but there is an alternative method where funds are moved automatically at the end of each day so that all but one account has a zero balance. In the example above, zero-balancing would work as shown in Table 4.3. The same amount of funds is available to the treasury as for the netting system, but funds actually move.

The choice of system depends upon the culture of the company involved. Zero-balancing implies a high degree of centralisation, but it also means that it can be more difficult for individual subsidiaries to track their own cash flow. There is also a widely held view that the introduction of a netting system within a group assists cash forecasting.

Bank agreements

If zero-balancing is to be used then written instructions will have to be given to the bank and signed on behalf of each subsidiary involved.

In netting systems, each subsidiary will be allocated a separate overdraft limit and there will be a net overdraft limit for the group. If each subsidiary is creditworthy then this might be, say, £20 million for each subsidiary, but only £5 million for the group overall. This will allow greater flexibility in day-to-day management. If particular subsidiaries are less creditworthy, then a guarantee or letter of comfort may be taken. This avoids the risk that all the borrowing ends up in the weakest company.

The bank may take a letter of set-off from all the companies involved, but increasingly full cross-guarantees from all companies are taken. This will allow the bank to set off credit and debit balances without notice. This provision is only likely to be used in insolvency, but it does allow the bank to use its own capital base effectively and therefore to offer higher overdraft limits to individual subsidiaries. Care should be taken that the set-off arrangement is approved by the board of each subsidiary, otherwise directors who were not party to the agreement might be able to sue those who did sign the agreement in the event that insolvency occurs and funds are transferred out of that particular subsidiary.

Multinational organisations

The same principles as apply in one country can be applied to a group of companies spread throughout a number of countries, but here the additional complications are those of currencies and the regulations of the countries involved. Centralisation of cash and payment management can provide a considerable number of benefits. These benefits might be:

- reduction of transaction costs;
- reduction of interest costs;
- greater buying power;
- reduction of exposures by matching;
- creating centres of excellence in terms of treasury staff;
- savings in tax;
- increasing management control, particularly in the area of policy.

For a multinational operation there is the key question of the location of the treasury centre. This does not have to be at the same place as the group head office and will depend upon the nature and flows of the group, as well as management culture. The key considerations for location are:

- taxation – it is often better to be based in a jurisdiction with favourable taxation arrangements, such as Dublin Docks, Belgium or the Netherlands, although the ability to integrate with the group's main business is also important;
- clear banking regulations in the country of the treasury centre;
- tax treaties from the treasury centre and head office to other countries where the group trades;

- good foreign exchange market;
- absence of exchange controls;
- availability of qualified treasury staff;
- the amount of group internal trade through that country;
- the culture of the group;
- the ability to supervise treasury staff.

In practice the greatest economies of scale will occur where all intra-group trade can be netted off at the centre, resulting in one net payment to each operating subsidiary, preferably either in one reference currency or in the currency of each operating subsidiary. This will result in the treasury centre carrying out a number of foreign exchange transactions with each operating subsidiary, but then having the benefit of netting the exposures at the centre and carrying out one main trade. In order to operate such a system efficiently, there will need to be a well established and controlled computer treasury management system. There are a number of such systems available and these should provide clear management reports as well as an automated confirmation system.

A note on currency

It is beyond the scope of this book to consider currency management in so far as it affects liquidity management. However, in the organisation of liquidity throughout a group, there are a number of techniques available to manage currency exposures. Above all, there must be a clear understanding of the purpose of liquidity management above any amount of currency management. The objective must be to have available the correct amount of currency in each location in which it is needed to be used to meet obligations as they fall due. Any attempt to net currency exposures which leaves an operating company without the necessary funds to pay suppliers will defeat the overall treasury objectives.

A common and practical way of managing currency exposures is leading and lagging. Leading is where a payment is made early and lagging is to delay payment. So cash-rich subsidiaries may pay early within the group either to allow other subsidiaries to avoid local financing costs or alternatively as a way of moving funds from depreciating currencies to stronger currencies. Lagging works in the opposite way.

However, care must be taken to consider the after-tax effect of such management techniques as well as ensuring that such methods comply with the relevant jurisdictions. Countries with high inflation and/or exchange controls will have restrictions available to prevent what they regard as abuse of the system.

Balance reporting systems

One of the central problems in cash management is obtaining enough information to make good decisions. Advances in technology now allow banks to provide PC based balance reporting systems. These allow companies access to both the nominal and cleared position on their bank accounts directly in their own offices. The use of a PC avoids manual intervention, allowing management to begin as early as desired, and also reduces the possibility of error. A typical example is shown in Table 4.4.

Details may often be pooled from different banks so that complete reports can be obtained and integrated into group reporting. The use of satellites and other communications networks can provide detailed reports worldwide in different currencies (Table 4.5). This level of detail can make much more sense of cash flow forecasts. In particular, the level of payments

Table 4.4 NatWest BankLine Plus balance report as at 30 April 1997. XYZ PLC Group

Account description	29 Apr 97 Closing ledger	29 Apr 97 Closing available	30 Apr 97 Current available	29 Apr 97 2 or more days' float
01497243(002)	600000–	600000–	600000–	0
XYZ PLC				
Treasury a/c				
01497189(005)	148634–	148634–	114305–	0
Parent company				
86571133(006)	373215	339017	387987	34198
Subsidiary Co No 1				
36486167(007)	442328	413492	452969	17336
Subsidiary Co No 2				
Net totals	66909	3875	126651	51534
Gross debits	748634–	748634–	714305–	0
Gross credits	815543	752509	840956	51534

clearing in the current day can be precise and if arrangements have been made for, say, next-day clearing of cash, a precise figure can be obtained. Varying levels of detail can be agreed with the bank. However, balance reporting systems will not pick up current-day transactions, which can include cheques presented across the counter.

Costs tend to be an initial fee followed by fixed monthly charges. The largest cost used to be the cost of the PC and printer, but for many businesses a PC they already own can also be used for balance reporting.

Banks constantly change the range of products available and it is often worth describing a problem to your banker in case there is a solution that could be adapted, but is not immediately obvious. It is useful to arrange for a system that can

Table 4.5 NatWest BankLine Plus previous day transaction report 29 Apr 1997. XYZ PLC Group

01497189 – Parent company

Credits posted

4 500.00	IPS2187081201099 Sumitomo Bank
118.63	BS571310040
427.16	Cash cheques
135.21	Div 1389933 Brt Ord shares

5 181.00

Debits posted

1 534.45	Chq 30574
1 244.83	Chq 30586
474.35	Chq 30576
27 650.00	TF group salaries
8 258.00	TF group pensions

39 161.63

interface with the main treasury system. Balance reporting and other treasury systems are developing fast, but they remain a management tool to aid decision-taking. The costs involved will allow not just a reduction of transactions, but also better decision-making, leading to better exposure management.

Conclusion

In summary, the relationship between a customer and its banker ideally can be a partnership. While there are many opportunities to negotiate and control costs, these can only be taken so far without undue consequences. However, banks have a role to play in providing information about the business in a form that the business can use.

5

The structure of interest rates and the yield curve

- The methods of quoting interest rates
- How to interpret what a particular interest rate means

Once we have established how much cash there is available to deposit or is needed to be borrowed, we can consider time-scales and the level of return we require. Recall, however, that return or cost should only be considered after liquidity considerations and the security of the investment have been taken into account. For the purposes of this chapter, let us assume that all possible investments are of equal risk so that the prime consideration is the absolute level of return.

The cash flow forecast will have indicated the length of time for which cash is available or required, but there are a wide range of decisions that can be taken in that period. Before exploring these, it is necessary to understand something about the structure of interest rates.

People are generally familiar with the concept that interest rates change all the time in the present world, but the personal experience tends to be limited to those occasions when there is a major shift brought about by a change in mortgage rates or savings account rates. These changes are relatively infrequent, more because of the costs of notifying changes and the associated marketing costs than because in the wholesale money-markets changes occur almost every minute. This is the essential feature of a floating interest rate.

Another general feature of the personal situation is that interest is not usually credited or charged on a daily basis, but at the end of a given period (say, annually) no matter what has happened to interest rates in the meantime.

In the wholesale markets, interest rates are usually quoted as a set rate for a given period, with interest paid at the end of that period. Thus, a rate might be quoted as:

1 month 11.5% pa

This means that, if we are talking about surplus funds, then for a deposit lasting 1 month, interest will be paid at the annual rate of 11.5% and the interest and principal will be repaid at the end of that month. Interest is calculated by using the actual number of days involved and assuming that a year has 365 days for sterling and 360 days for most other currencies.

Hence, in this example if the deposit were £1 million and the exact number of days was 31, then the total interest would be:

$$1\,000\,000 \times 11.5/100 \times 31/365 = £9767.12$$

But if the deposit was $1\,000\,000, then the interest calculation would be:

$$1\,000\,000 \times 11.5/100 \times 31/360 = \$9902.78$$

It is also important to remember that different instruments quote their interest rates on different bases and therefore they would need to be compared on an equivalent basis. These bases are described later in this chapter.

Bid and offer

Naturally, the same rates are not quoted for both deposits and borrowing. If a bank is looking for deposits then it will bid for those deposits; if it is looking to lend to another bank (that is, place a deposit with another bank), then it will offer. This gives rise to the concept of bid and offer rates. These might be quoted as follows:

Overnight	$11\frac{1}{8}-11$
7 days	$11\frac{1}{16}-11$
1 month	$11-10\frac{1}{2}$
3 months	$10\frac{7}{8}-10\frac{3}{4}$
6 months	$10\frac{11}{16}-10\frac{5}{8}$

(Note that these are all per annum rates.) Thus a bank will agree to take deposits at $10\frac{3}{4}\%$ pa for 3 months fixed, or will lend (to other prime banks) at $11\frac{1}{16}\%$ pa for 7 days.

LIBOR and basis points

The rates that are quoted above represent the rates at which prime banks would be prepared to deal with each other. For weaker banks or for companies, rates will tend to be higher than the offer rate. Equally, since prime banks tend to be strong and can therefore attract deposits more easily, they tend to have lower bid rates.

The offer rate used by major international banks is known as LIBOR (the London inter-bank offered rate), i.e. the rate at which a bank is prepared to place a deposit with (that is, lend to) a prime bank. LIBOR tends to be the benchmark rate for

75

wholesale money-market dealings worldwide, not just in London. There will be a different LIBOR for different currencies and also each bank will set its own LIBOR.

There are also related rates: LIBID represents the rate at which a bank is willing to accept a deposit and LIMEAN is the average of a given pair of LIBID and LIBOR.

There are also rates used, based on financial centres other than London, such as PIBOR for Paris, FIBOR for Frankfurt. These are particularly relevant for local currencies, but the use of modern technology should mean that rates converge very quickly.

Interest on loans is often quoted over LIBOR – for banks this represents their profit margin as well as the costs of complying with the capital adequacy requirements of the Bank of England and other central banks. The margin over LIBOR may be expressed as so many percentage points, e.g. $\frac{1}{2}\%$ pa or it may be expressed as a given number of basis points. A basis point is $\frac{1}{100}\%$ pa, so $\frac{1}{2}\%$ is the same as 50 basis points. This terminology has become more popular as banks have moved away from quoting in sixteenths and eighths and now use 5 or 10 basis points (or, of course, any number; for certain large deals as small as 1 or 2).

Interest rates and the yield to maturity

There are a whole range of instruments that can be used for short term investment which have different conventions on when interest is paid. The separation between the money-markets which used to cover instruments of less than 1 year and the international capital markets is all but gone. Sophisticated investors are able to move between markets and instruments easily, particularly with the range of derivatives available to manage interest rate risk.

When comparing instruments it is critical to understand when interest is paid. Some instruments pay interest every 6 months, others on fixed dates, and others claim to carry no interest but offer the return by an increase in capital value. For example, 2 instruments both with quoted interest rates (sometimes called the 'coupon') of 10% may not actually provide the same total return. If one pays interest annually and the other semi-annually, then the investor in the one with semi-annual interest payments will get the better deal as he or she can reinvest the first interest payment at the end of 6 months. However, in general money-market instruments pay interest on maturity unless they last for longer than a year, in which case interest is also paid annually (see Chapter 4).

Capital market instruments such as bonds also operate on different bases, so Eurobonds pay interest annually on a 360-day year basis, but domestic sterling bonds pay interest semi-annually on a 365-day year basis.

Active investors do not tend to invest in a straightforward instrument and leave it at that – they also manage the yield by using derivatives (see Chapter 8) and these all have different conventions on when cash actually moves.

When comparing two instruments, or indeed a combination of instruments, it is necessary to compare them on a common basis and the way to do this is to set out all the cash flows involved and then discount them. Whilst it is relatively straightforward to identify the cash flows, the discount factor needs some care. For short term instruments the best approach would be to identify the yield in the form of the internal rate of return (in effect the discount factor that gives a net present value of zero). Remember that if returns for similar levels of risk are very different, then there is something amiss, as modern technology allows transparency between markets.

For longer dated instruments the best method of comparing them is to calculate the yield to maturity. This is the rate, expressed as a percentage, that discounts all future payments of interest, principal repayments and other cash flows back to their present value or market price.

Total yield

Naturally, in spite of the discussion of the alternative rates available, it is the absolute level of return or cost which becomes important (assuming a consistent exposure to credit risk).

Another factor to be evaluated in the selection of interest periods is the comparison of the returns available from different maturities. Thus, we need to establish how to compare 10.5% pa with interest paid quarterly with 11% pa with interest paid annually. The basic method is to put them on to a common basis of the total return (or cost) over a full year. The use of a year also matches most company reporting periods and thus will be the measure most familiar to other colleagues.

In the case of 10.5% with interest quarterly, the total return is going to be

$$\left(1+\frac{0.105}{4}\right)^4 = 1.1092$$

i.e. the total return is 10.92%. This means that on an investment of £1 million, the total return would be approximately £109 200. This can be confirmed as follows:

Interest at end of first quarter $=£$ 26 250
Interest on £1 026 250 at end of second quarter $=£$ 26 939
Interest on £1 053 189 at end of third quarter $=£$ 27 646
Interest on £1 080 835 at end of fourth quarter $=£$ 28 371

i.e. a total return of £109 206. This would be compared with a yield of 11% in the case of annual interest and, assuming constant expectations of interest rates, the return from 11% would be higher. As with the interpretation of the yield curve (see below), this can be but part of the information on which to base a decision.

Note that the general formula for the yield of an instrument with nominal interest rate of r (quoted as r% pa), but with interest paid after d days on the basis of a 365-day year (see above) is:

$$\left(1 + \frac{rd}{36\,500}\right)^{\frac{365}{d}}$$

The answer will be quoted as $1.x$ where x is the resultant yield. Naturally this formula assumes that reinvestment will be available at the same rate at the end of d days, but that is all part of the central problem.

In order to give a general feel, Table 5.1 lists various yields with the compared quoted rates. So, it is useful to note that approximately 11.5% pa quoted for a 3-month rate will give a total return of 12% pa.

Yield and the yield curve

If the yields on comparable instruments for given periods are plotted on a graph against time then this will give a curve

Table 5.1 Various yields compared with quoted rates

Months	Yield (%)				
	9	10	11	12	15
1	8.65	9.57	10.48	11.39	14.06
2	8.68	9.61	10.53	11.44	14.14
3	8.71	9.65	10.57	11.49	14.22
6	8.81	9.77	10.71	11.66	14.48
12	9.00	10.00	11.00	12.00	15.00

known as the yield curve. A yield curve can be for any period, lasting up to 20 years and beyond. Instruments are considered comparable if they have similar characteristics and there are two main issues that may make them different:

1 *Credit risk.* It is obvious that an investor in unrated corporate paper will seek a higher return than the holder of US treasury bonds to compensate for the additional risk.
2 *Liquidity risk.* Government bonds tend to be issued in larger amounts than corporate bonds, offering greater liquidity to investors. Liquidity is also affected by the number of market makers prepared to make a market in the bond or security.

Therefore, when preparing a yield curve, it is important to ensure that only securities that have comparable credit and liquidity features should be compared. The easiest starting-point is to strip out these factors and use government securities (say US treasury bills for US dollars and gilts for sterling). This will produce the *risk-free yield curve*.

The basic shape of the yield curve will tell us in general terms what the market is expecting to happen to interest rates. There are three main shapes of the yield curve: normal or positive, flat, and negative or inverse.

Normal or positive

In this case, rates are progressively higher for longer periods (Figure 5.1). In a stable interest rate environment this should occur naturally for three reasons:

1 *The effect of compound interest.* If we deposited for 3 months, collected the interest and re-deposited for 3 months at the same rate, we would end up with a greater amount than if we had just deposited at that rate for 6 months at the outset.
2 *Liquidity preference.* If we are offered the same effective return over two different periods, then, all other things being equal, we would choose the shorter period as it provides greater flexibility.
3 *Credit risk.* The longer the period of investment, the greater the chance of default. This is clearly a more significant factor over the very long term.

The positive yield curve will be steepest when interest rates are expected to rise.

Flat

In this case, the interest rates quoted are broadly the same over all periods being considered (Figure 5.2). This yield curve can

Yield %

Maturity (months/years)

5.1 Normal yield curve.

5.2   Flat yield curve.

arise as a result of changing investor perceptions. As investors move from periods of expectation of rising to falling interest rates, they may become indifferent to the maturity in which they make their investment. Technically, because of the effect of compound interest, rates would be expected to fall over time.

Inverse

In this case quoted rates are generally falling over the periods of the curve (Figure 5.3).

5.3   Inverse yield curve.

All of the above curves require interpretation, specifically to understand what the market is expecting to happen. Two other shapes that may occur are:

1 *Hump-backed*, where investors expect lower rates in the longer term, preceded by increases in the medium term. This shape may also arise because of an anomaly where certain maturities were particularly cheap.

2 *Trough* or *inverted hump-backed*, which is the inverse of the hump-backed yield curve.

Disaggregation

If we are quoted 12% for a 3-month investment and also 12% for a 6-month investment then, all other things being equal, it would be logical to choose to invest for 3 months and then reinvest in 3 months to gain the benefits of compounding. If this were the situation, one could deduce that the market anticipates that rates will be lower for 3 months in 3 months' time, otherwise everybody would be making money this way.

By removing the effects of compounding or disaggregating then we can calculate what the market expects rates to be for 3 months in 3 months' time. Assuming equal whole months, the interest for 3 months and 6 months respectively on £1 million at 12% is £30000 and £60000.

So what rate would produce £30000 for the second 3 months on a deposit of £1030000? The answer is 11.65%, i.e. the market expects the 3-month rate in 3 months' time to be 11.65%.

The formula for the general case is:

$$\left(1+i_m\right)\left(1+i_n\right)=\left(1+i_{m+n}\right)$$

where: i is the interest rate pa for a given period expressed as a fraction (so 12% pa will be $\frac{12}{100}$) and adjusted for the proportion of the year (so a 12% pa rate for a 6 month period will be $\frac{12}{100} \times \frac{6}{12}$), i_m the interest rate i for the period m, i_n the interest rate i for the period n and i_{m+n} is the interest rate i for the period formed by extending the period m by the period n. In practice the actual number of days involved would be used as would a precise 360- or 365-day year, depending upon the currency involved. Again, instead of using $\frac{6}{12}$, a precise calculation might use $\frac{183}{360}$.

So, in the above case m is 3, n is 3 and $m + n$ is 6. If we were to calculate the 12% example this way, it would be:

$$\left(1 + 0.12 \times \frac{3}{12}\right) \times \left(1 + x \times \frac{3}{12}\right) = \left(1 + 0.12 \times \frac{6}{12}\right)$$

or

$$1.03 \times \left(1 + x \times \frac{3}{12}\right) = 1.06$$

so

$$x = \left(\frac{1.06}{1.03} - 1\right) \times \frac{12}{3}$$

$$= 0.1165$$

or

$$11.65\% \text{ pa}$$

Using the rates given above in the section on bid and offer on page 75 we can calculate what the market expects 3-month rates to be in 3 months' time in the same way. Thus:

$$\left(1 + 0.1075 \times \frac{3}{12}\right) \times \left(1 + x \times \frac{3}{12}\right) = \left(1 + 0.10625 \times \frac{6}{12}\right)$$

or

$$1.026875 \times \left(1 + \frac{x}{4}\right) = 1.053125$$

so

$$x = 0.102252$$

or

$$10.2252\% \text{ pa}$$

This disaggregated rate is also known as the *forward forward rate*. The forward forward rate is an important element of interest rate risk management. This market view of what the market expects rates will be in the future is central to making judgements. Other markets have developed from the basic forward forward such as the FRA and interest rate futures markets. These are discussed in Chapter 8.

Selecting an interest period

If there is a sum available for deposit for 6 months and the rates above are quoted, how can an interest period be chosen? One obvious alternative is to deposit for 6 months at $10\frac{5}{8}\%$ pa. But a different choice might be to deposit for 3 months at $10\frac{3}{4}\%$ and then re-deposit at the end of 3 months. The real problem is that we do not know for certain what interest rates are going to be in 3 months' time. Naturally, we can form our own judgement but we can also look at what the market expects to happen to interest rates by calculating the forward forward rate by looking at the yield curve. In practice rate screens such as Reuters will quote these rates in the form of an FRA price (see Chapter 8).

However, investment decisions are usually not that straightforward. Increasingly we may be presented with complex instruments with cash flows arising on non-standard dates, say in 42 days and 75 days. How can decisions be made between such instruments? The way to do this is to discount the various cash flows by reference to rates available in the market. The problem is choosing the discount factor to apply. The choice of discount factor is resolved by selecting the correct yield curve – the zero coupon yield curve. For more straightforward comparisons, we can also look at the forward yield curve.

The zero coupon and forward yield curves

As we have seen, the basic yield curve is a graphical representation of the yield on an instrument plotted against time, say sterling LIBOR. However, the yield curve considered so far makes two critical assumptions:

1 That the investment is trading at par – i.e. there is no capital gain.
2 That cash flows (usually interest) received can be reinvested at the same rate.

In short term investment management it is relatively straightforward to deal with the first issue as we can think of investing an amount and receiving an interest rate relative to the amount invested. For other instruments, such as treasury bills or gilts, then the capital growth can be factored into any discounting. However, if we invest in an instrument for one year which pays interest 6-monthly, then in order to consider it against another instrument, we have to assume that the interest can be reinvested at the same rate. This has been addressed so far by considering the forward forward rate. This is a representation of the market's current expectations of future rates for single periods; it does not deal with the complexities of interest received meanwhile. For this the zero coupon curve is necessary.

The zero coupon curve represents the rate at which a *single* cash flow at each particular maturity should be discounted to give today's present value. In order to demonstrate how this operates, consider that instruments trading at par have been quoted at the following rates:

Year	Yield
1	5%
2	5.5%
3	6.25%

Also assume that interest is paid annually on each instrument.

For the first year, the zero coupon yield is the same as the par yield, i.e. 5%. This is because there is only one cash flow which arises on maturity.

To calculate the 2-year zero coupon rate, there are two steps. First, value the cash flow arising at the end of the first year, i.e. 0.055. This is then discounted at the 1-year zero coupon rate of 5%:

$$0.055 \times \frac{1}{1+0.05} = 0.05238$$

This will leave $1 - 0.05238 = 0.94762$ of the remaining cash flow. At the end of the second year, we will receive the principal of the 2-year instrument plus the second lot of interest, i.e. 1.055, so the 2-year zero coupon rate, i, is going to be:

$$(1+i)^2 \times 0.94762 = 1.055$$

which solves to $i = 5.514\%$.

Take the same approach to the third year. The cash flows to consider are 0.0625, 0.0625 and 1.0625, so:

- discount 0.0625 at 5% to give a present value of 0.05952;
- discount 0.0625 at 5.514% for 2 years to give a present value of 0.05614;
- this leaves $1 - 0.05952 - 0.05614 = 0.88434$ which, when applied to the final cash flow of 1.0625 for 3 years, produces a 3-year zero rate of 6.309%.

So, in order to plot the zero coupon curve for this instrument, rates of 5%, 5.514% and 6.309% would be plotted against 1, 2 and 3 years respectively.

Notice that the zero coupon yield is not the same as the forward forward. Considering 2 years, the anticipated rate for 1 year in 1 year's time, i, is calculated by:

$$(1.05) \times (1+i) = (1.055)^2 - \text{giving } i \text{ of } 6\%.$$

For simple comparisons, it is possible to look at the forward yield curve. This is a curve of forward forward rates starting on a certain forward date – e.g. for a curve starting in 3 months' time, plot a 1-month rate starting in 3 months' time, followed by the 2-month rate starting in 3 months' time and so on (using

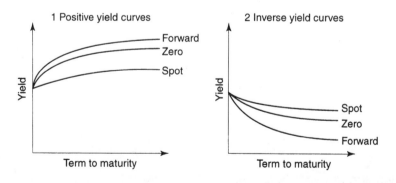

5.4 The relationship between spot, zero and forward yield curves.

88

FRA terminology, this is the graph plotting 3v4, 3v5, 3v6 and so on – see Chapter 8).

The relationship between the spot, zero and forward yield curves in positive and inverse yield curve environments can be shown as in Figure 5.4.

Interpreting the yield curve and taking a view on rates

From the example of 12% for both 3 and 6 months, we can deduce that a flat yield curve means that the market expects interest rates to fall over time. Consequently, an inverse yield curve means that interest rates are expected to fall more sharply over the period.

In the case of a normal yield curve, the degree of the slope becomes important. If the slope is very gentle, interest rates may still be expected to fall, but a steeper slope might mean that market expectations are for interest rates to remain broadly stable and steeper slopes still to increase. The choice of yield curve can now be understood depending upon the use to which it will be put. Quotations on these bases are now readily available using appropriate computer software.

The general understanding of the shape of the yield curve lets the treasurer make broad decisions on the period of investment or borrowing to be selected. But first the treasurer will need to have his or her own view on interest rates. Thus, presented with a flat yield curve but the belief that interest rates will rise, an investor will select a short period, anticipating an increase in rates.

The efficient market hypothesis would imply that the treasurer should have no reason to believe that rates should be any different from those implied by the yield curve and that the period to be selected should match the period for which funds are available or required. In practice, there are a number of reasons why this does not take place. First, people will take different views and this is especially so in particularly volatile markets. There may be more liquidity in the more common periods of 3 or 6 months which could provide times where rates do not match precisely those expected by the market for other interest periods. More commonly, however, it is by no means clear for how long the funds are available or required, or indeed it may be for such a long period that consecutive shorter periods have to be chosen. Given this situation, there is a need to take active decisions on interest periods, and the combination of the yield curve and the treasurer's own view of interest rates will form the major basis for the decision (along with amount and the actual period of surplus or requirement).

The treasurer can form a view by taking appropriate economic research from banks as well as by reading widely in the appropriate newspapers such as the *Financial Times* or the *Wall Street Journal*. It is important to know when key pieces of economic news are due to be released as these may affect the supply and demand in the market for particular interest rates. Interest rates in the long term are affected by the level of economic activity and also by government or central bank policy and intervention. Increasingly the cash market is affected by prices quoted in the futures market and advice should be obtainable from dealers when large positions are building in the futures market that might affect the timing of any decision.

Risk

Whilst treasurers will have their own view on the direction of interest rates, there will have to be a limit to the degree they can take a view that is too far out of step with the market. (Certain investors, notably hedge funds, make their return from accepting a very high level of risk precisely sometimes by taking contrary views.) Indeed, in some situations even if the treasurer agrees with the market view, he or she may not be able to take *any* risk that the market moves the other way because of the impact on the business. One such situation where the anticipation of rising or falling rates is not the dominant factor is when a company (or an individual, for that matter) cannot afford the consequences in cash terms of rates rising or falling below a particular level. This might be because the additional interest cost (in the case of a borrower) could not be serviced and the company forced into liquidation. Alternatively, a company that derives a high proportion of its profit from interest income might be unwilling to risk a reduction in profit. This might mean that whatever the treasurer's own views on interest rates, a safe policy may need to be adopted by choosing longer periods to secure particular interest rates. This question will be examined in greater depth in Chapter 7.

Above all, a regular examination of the implications of the yield curve should alert the treasurer to the degree of interest rate risk.

Different interest rate bases

As has been mentioned, different instruments have different bases on which to calculate interest. The most common difference is that sterling yields are quoted on the basis of a 365-day year, whereas most other currencies are quoted on the basis of a 360-day year. Some methods of quoting yields assume annual interest, others assume semi-annual interest. Therefore, when comparing yields quoted on different instruments it is very important to ensure that the rates are being quoted on the same basis.

There are 4 major ways that yield might be quoted:

1 Money-market yield (MMY).
2 Bond equivalent yield (BEY).
3 Discount.
4 ISMA (sometimes called AIBD) yield.

These will now be described.

Money-market yield

This assumes a 360-day year basis and is used for short term instruments. It is basically straightforward. If I earn $5000 on an investment of $500000 for 150 days, the MMY is:

$$\frac{5000}{500000} \times \frac{360}{150} \times 100 = 2.4\% \text{ pa}$$

Note: always use 360 in the numerator, but the actual number of days in the denominator.

MMY is used for:

- US$ LIBOR;
- Euro commercial paper (except sterling);
- Euro certificates of deposit.

Bond equivalent yield

This is the same approach as for MMY, except that 365 is used instead of 360, so for an investment of £500000 which offers a return of £5000 after 150 days, the BEY is:

$$\frac{5000}{500000} \times \frac{365}{150} \times 100 = 2.433\% \text{ pa}$$

BEY is used for:

- sterling LIBOR;
- gilts;
- sterling certificates of deposit;
- sterling commercial paper;
- sterling corporate bonds;
- US treasury notes (precisely these are quoted as actual days/ actual days – so use 366 instead of 365 in a leap year).

Discount

Some instruments, notably bankers' acceptances (see Chapter 6), are quoted at a discount. For example, a bill rate might be quoted as 6%, but if you aim to borrow £1 000 000 because of the discount effect, you would actually only receive £940 000 (assuming the borrowing was for 1 year). This will have the effect of making the actual rate of borrowing on a yield basis (either MMY or BEY) higher than the quoted discount rate.

ISMA (or AIBD) yield

None of the methods of quoting yields so far discussed has taken the effect of compounding interest into account. So, for example, some instruments might assume interest is paid annually, others more frequently. The purpose of the ISMA yield is to ensure that the yield is quoted to include the frequency of interest payments. This is the approach described earlier in this chapter on the basis of total yields. So, depending on the use of

360 or 365 days, the formula to convert from a stated MMY or BEY is:

$$\left\{\left(1+\frac{i}{n}\right)^{n}-1\right\}\times100$$

where i is the stated MMY or BEY and n is the number of compounding periods involved. So, if an instrument with semi-annual interest is quoted with a rate of 6%, the ISMA yield is $(1.03)^{2}-1$, i.e. 6.09%. Notice that the rate is higher to reflect the opportunity to reinvest the first semi-annual interest payment.

This basis of yield is used frequently by professional investors – ISMA stands for the International Securities Markets Association (AIBD is the Association of International Bond Dealers).

The formulae for converting between these interest rate bases are given in the Appendix, p 188.

We will look at the instruments for which these yields are quoted in Chapter 6.

6

Liquidity and the use of deposit and borrowing instruments

- A brief description of various short term deposit and borrowing instruments
- How to decide which instrument is appropriate for a given circumstance

The management of liquidity will give rise to cash surpluses or requirements and these will need to be invested or borrowed through the use of money-market instruments. The choice of a particular instrument will affect the *availability* of liquidity. For example, investing in an instrument which cannot be sold in the market and is only available on maturity (say, a 1-year fixed deposit) means that that amount of liquidity is not available. Similarly, in borrowing facilities, the availability of a committed line of credit (as opposed to an uncommitted line or an overdraft) means that liquidity is available, even if the line of credit is not drawn. This chapter considers the general characteristics of instruments so that a decision can be taken on whether an instrument is likely to suit a particular requirement. Individual features are described; however, care should be taken to understand how these operate in any particular market and how they have evolved.

95

Given the concentration on liquidity, the instruments considered are generally short term (i.e. with maturities of less than 1 year) but, as will be seen, borrowing facilities with maturities of greater than 1 year are frequently part of planning for future liquidity.

Deposit instruments

The need to deposit will have been identified from a cash flow forecast. This will also have identified the amount available and the period for which the funds are forecast to be available, and clearly these requirements will colour the selection of instrument. The cash forecast will also allow a judgement on the risk that the cash may be required sooner than planned (for example, there is a 50% possibility that cash may be needed sooner). The main objectives of short term investment described in Chapter 1 will also be important:

- safety;
- liquidity;
- profitability.

(Note that the order in which these objectives is set out is critical. If a different priority is given to profitability, say, then there is the risk of total loss for a higher theoretical short term gain.) Other issues which are also important are:

- flexibility;
- risk diversification.

One of the most common types of problem in short term depositing is the situation where funds are thought to be available for a given period, say 6 months, but there is a chance that they might be required sooner, say after 3 months. One way of dealing with this issue is to deposit for 3 months and then see what the position is like then. Alternatively, a 6-month instrument in which there is a liquid market could be selected if the return available seems particularly suitable. (A fuller consideration of this type of question is given in Chapter 7.)

We will look at each of these issues in turn.

Safety

There is no great benefit if a deposit earns a higher return and yet is not repaid in full on maturity. For any deposit counterparty there should be an approved internal credit limit which sets out both a maximum amount to be exposed and also a maximum maturity. Risk analysis will start from prime sovereign risk (say, US treasury bills or UK gilts) and then expand through either external credit ratings or internal analysis to establish an acceptable level of risk. Care should be taken over generalisations – recall the collapses (in different circumstances) of both BCCI and Barings. Different risk levels may be considered as between financial and corporate counterparties – so a much higher exposure may be acceptable for a leading UK clearing bank than for a prime corporation.

A further type of risk that arises is that of market risk. For some marketable securities, there is a risk that, if realised prior to maturity, the capital value is less than at the point of investment. This is especially true of fixed interest securities where some of the movement in rates is reflected in the price of the security.

In general, there is a trade-off between risk and reward. If two comparable securities are offering different returns, then it is likely that the security offering the higher return has higher risk. So:

- for equal returns an investor will prefer lower risk;
- for higher risk an investor will require a higher return.

When considering an investment opportunity, the level of acceptable risk must be considered first. As has been stressed, a higher yield of, say, $\frac{1}{2}$% pa can easily be wiped out by the failure of the investment. Even if security is offered, there will be time delay and cost in the recovery of that security.

Liquidity

When applied to an investment liquidity is the ability to convert that investment into cash. If a company has alternative sources of liquidity (such as available borrowing facilities) then an illiquid investment can be considered. Also, the certainty of the cash flow is important. If it is absolutely clear that the funds may be invested for a fixed term, then liquidity is of lesser importance. So, if a company has $10 million to invest and the most that may be required is $4 million, then $6 million may be invested in an illiquid investment, such as a fixed term deposit.

Again there is an inverse relationship between liquidity and yield as liquid investments offer lower yields than illiquid investments for similar risk and other characteristics. This is known as liquidity preference.

Profitability

Only when the issues of security and liquidity have been addressed can profitability be considered. Clearly, investors will naturally seek the greatest profitability. Given interest rate volatility in international markets, the real advantage in profitability arises from timing and maturity considerations rather than the choice between individual instruments.

98

Flexibility

The liquidity of an instrument offers one form of flexibility. However, many instruments used for investment and interest rate management can only be traded either in fixed amounts or for specific maturities (e.g. financial futures). Companies' cash flows are all different and the flexibility offered by being able to trade for a particular amount to a specific date that suits the company is important.

Risk diversification

Risk is considered in greater detail in the next chapter. However, for corporations with large amounts to invest, it is appropriate to diversify those investments. This may be:

- across individual banks and other corporations on an individual basis;
- across sectors;
- across instruments and maturities.

The diversification between organisations and sectors avoids the risk of concentration of risk in terms of credit. However, diversifying across instruments and maturities lowers the risk against market moves both in terms of profitability and also in terms of the availability of markets for reinvestment when the investment matures.

Individual instruments and markets for investment will now be described in terms of these features.

Bank deposits

Deposits with banks can be made either with the company's usual bank or through the wholesale markets with a different bank. In any event, the first requirement is to be satisfied with the credit standing of the bank (or, technically, other financial institutions such as building societies, licensed deposit-takers, savings and loans, etc). As the collapse of BCCI graphically showed, it is irresponsible to rely on just the advice of any third party, whether a broker or a central bank, unless that third party has given a formal guarantee. Further, for large sums, credit limits should be set in order to diversify risk.

The maturity of the deposit will be established at the time it is placed together with the rate of interest. Certainly, call deposits (that is, ones that may be withdrawn at no notice) will be available, but the return is likely to be that much lower. Therefore, call deposits are only suitable for smaller sums unsuitable for the wholesale markets.

Fixed term deposits will be of the basic type considered in Chapter 5, i.e. they will be for the given period with interest usually paid on maturity (although, for periods of greater than 6 months, interest may be paid 6-monthly). Also, other than in exceptional circumstances, they will not be repaid until the end of the period. Thus, if there is a chance that the funds will be required before the stated maturity of the deposit, then either a liquid instrument should have been chosen or a shorter period, or other sources of liquidity (e.g. borrowing facilities) should be available.

The depth of the wholesale money-markets in the major currencies means that there is considerable flexibility available as to amounts and maturities from overnight through to 5 years. Deals are mainly struck from the current day, although future start dates are also available. Usually the minimum amount dealt is £250000 for sterling or $250000 for US dollars, with the best quotes available for 1 million (of either $ or £) and above.

- *Safety*. Depends upon the bank with which the deposit is placed.
- *Liquidity*. Deposits tend to be for fixed terms and therefore they are illiquid.
- *Profitability*. These deposits (via LIBOR) tend to be the benchmark against which other investments may be measured. Yield will also depend upon the risk of the individual bank.
- *Flexibility*. Deposits can be for any amount (subject to very large amounts) and for individually selected dates (with less ease over 1 year).

Certificates of deposit

A certificate of deposit (CD) is a negotiable bearer instrument certificate issued by a bank or building society evidencing a deposit. These certificates may be traded in a fairly active secondary market and are priced as a function of the principal invested, the stated return on the CD and current money-market interest rates.

Banks have issued CDs since 1968 and other institutions such as UK building societies and savings & loans in the US also issue CDs. A CD may theoretically be sold at any date up to its maturity. However, the liquidity of any particular CD will depend upon the quality of the issuer. Many banks hold each others' CDs as part of their own liquidity management. CDs are available for periods up to 5 years (although they are less common above 1 year) and can be quoted on either a fixed rate or floating rate basis. For very short term CDs there is no difference, but for longer periods floating rate CDs have their coupon reset every 6 months. (In this sense floating rate CDs are similar to floating rate notes which are debt obligations issued by banks or corporations.) The interest rate payable upon maturity by the issuing institution is often lower than that available from a direct deposit because of the liquidity of the CD and may be up to $\frac{3}{8}$% pa below LIBID.

Although CDs offer useful liquidity, it is still preferable to anticipate holding them until maturity because of the risk of capital loss if they are sold prior to maturity. This capital loss arises usually because of the movement in interest rates. The liquidity of a particular CD depends upon the issuer. In the UK those of the clearing banks are most liquid; other banks' CDs are traded on a name-by-name basis and are often less liquid and therefore higher yielding. Likewise, in the USA, CDs issued by the major US banks offer greatest liquidity.

- *Safety*. Dependent upon the issuer, but note there is market risk if CDs are sold prior to maturity.
- *Liquidity*. This is the essential feature.
- *Profitability*. Lower than for bank deposits to compensate for the greater liquidity.
- *Flexibility*. CDs are issued in set amounts and for dates that suit the issuer. However, investors can enter the market at dates that suit them and plan to sell the CDs prior to maturity.

Local authority and government bonds

These often have the liquidity characteristics of CDs, but the market for a particular issue may in itself not be particularly liquid. The returns available will vary by issue and, as always, the credit risk needs to be assessed. However, government risk is likely to be prime for any given currency. Care needs to be taken with local authorities given the potential for bankruptcy in certain US situations (recall New York City) and the concern over debt levels and the question of *ultra vires* in the UK – although this is much less of an issue now. The most familiar government investments are gilts in the UK and treasury bills in the USA.

Commercial paper

Commercial paper (CP) is a debt instrument issued by a company for a given period and with a fixed face value. The paper is issued at a discount to the face value representing the effective interest rate. Commercial paper is a form of *disintermediation* in that banks, if involved, act as brokers and arrangers and do not lend themselves. This market has developed as banks have sought not to lend themselves, given the constraints on their balance sheets. There are three major markets:

1 The Euro commercial paper market (ECP).
2 The sterling commercial paper market (SCP).
3 The US domestic commercial paper market (USCP).

Each market will appeal to different investors and issuers, depending upon the level of regulation involved, the currency involved and the liquidity of the market. USCP is pre-eminent amongst short term promissory note markets and has existed since 1820. The markets in Europe are much more recent. At the end of 1995 there was nearly US$700 billion outstanding in USCP compared with $87 billion in ECP.

Typical returns are likely to be higher than for comparable bank deposits (other than for the most creditworthy multinational corporations) and this reflects the increased credit risk. Most investors will not have the skills or resources available to undertake the necessary regular credit evaluation, therefore CP programmes are frequently rated by credit-rating agencies such as Moody's, IBCA or Standard & Poor's. Investments might then only be made in CP issued by companies with a specified rating or better. This would not remove the credit risk.

Commercial paper can be liquid, but this depends upon the state of the market and, often, the quality of the issuer.

- *Safety*. This will depend upon the issuer and care needs to be taken. Many investors rely upon a rating (say A1/P1).
- *Liquidity*. Depending upon the depth of the issue, CP may be liquid.
- *Profitability*. Depends upon the quality of the issuer, but would normally be higher than for bank deposits. Yield increases with risk.
- *Flexibility*. As for CDs.

Bills of exchange

A bill of exchange is again an instrument evidencing a debt obligation, and bills of exchange were the traditional method of securing extended credit in international trade. The underlying credit risk on a bill rests with the obligor on the bill, but this may be enhanced by a financial institution accepting the bill (cf bankers' acceptances).

Bills may be traded and they are priced on a discounted basis. In the UK, bills of exchange which have been accepted by prime banks are known as eligible bills. Eligible bills form one of the ways by which the Bank of England influences short term interest rates. Rates may often be attractive and an active market in eligible bills is maintained by the discount houses and certain other financial institutions. The rate of return available may sometimes be better than for an equivalent CD.

Ineligible bills tend to attract higher interest rates, but the risk is frequently greater and the market less liquid.

- *Safety*. Safety depends on credit of issuer or the accepting bank.
- *Liquidity*. Eligible bills are more liquid than ineligible bills.
- *Flexibility*. Depends upon the range available.
- *Profitability*. Tends to be better than CDs, but is linked to the credit of the issuer.

Different currencies

Before considering borrowing instruments, the issue of investment in different currencies should be touched upon. Throughout, it has been assumed that investments have been made in one currency with a requirement for returns in that currency. It is clearly possible to introduce a further degree of risk and seek higher returns by speculating on the future movement of exchange rates. Thus, a higher nominal return in a particular currency could be sought if the investor believed that that currency would not depreciate by more than the relative interest rate differential. But this needs to be a conscious decision and in considering liquidity management at this level it is best to remain in one currency and make decisions on that basis. If the necessary skills are available and the risk is deemed to be acceptable, then this is a further area of opportunity.

Infrequently, it is possible to sell the surplus currency spot for a different currency, invest in that currency and sell the total proceeds in the forward foreign exchange market to achieve a return greater than investing in the original currency. This is known as *covered arbitrage*. The efficient operation of the markets, together with dealing spreads and costs, make these opportunities rare and when they occur, they do not last very long.

Obtaining and selling deposit instruments

Having selected the type of instrument that most suits a given investment need, the same issues arise as are often the case when buying any product. Where can I buy it and how much will it cost?

For the small business, the clearing bank is the natural place to start. Naturally it will offer its own products but an element of competition may be introduced by approaching a second bank. For small transactions it is often impractical and costly to shop around too much.

For larger transactions it is sensible to approach one of the banks' central dealing rooms. Here up-to-the-minute quotes may be obtained and consequently the most competitive price or interest rate. Transactions are all carried out over the telephone and are confirmed in writing afterwards. Competing quotes can thus be obtained from a number of banks for large transactions. In the USA, the largest issuers of CP issue their own CP directly and do not need to appoint dealers. The use of banks and other traders will allow access to secondary markets, that is, instruments traded after their initial issue. The use of a secondary market should provide a firm assessment of current market prices.

A number of banks will trade in CDs and CP, if these are the favoured instruments. There are also a number of firms of money-brokers in the UK. Their role is to match borrowers and depositors and earn their return by deducting a commission (usually from the borrower). They do not take any credit risk themselves, nor do they offer advice (as local authorities in the UK have realised following the collapse of BCCI) .

It is often sensible to start with the company's own clearing or merchant bank before going out too widely if the particular arrangements for an instrument are unfamiliar. However, investors should always be clear about the liquidity of a particular instrument when buying it – that is, can it be sold before maturity (and, if so, how?) or does it have to be (or is it preferable to be) held until maturity?

Borrowing instruments

The essential feature of borrowing as it affects liquidity is the availability of borrowed funds when they are required. The consideration of borrowing instruments in this book looks at the marginal borrowing facilities. It does not look at structural long term debt such as institutional debt or long term committed facilities as these are fundamental to the basic capital structure decision facing any company.

The same principles broadly apply to borrowing to manage liquidity as apply to depositing.

- *Safety*. Safety does not apply in the same way as for depositing. However, there is little point in arranging a borrowing facility from a bank that fails and leaves the borrower without the intended facilities.
- *Liquidity*. The *availability* of the facilities is critical. The difference between committed and uncommitted facilities is discussed below. However, care should be taken to ensure that facilities are available for both the amount and the period intended. Large, profitable companies in major economies will have access to many sources of finance, but for companies in developing economies operating within tight monetary policy or for growing companies, this is an important issue.
- *Flexibility*. The ability to choose to borrow right to the exact figure is important. Thus, although overdrafts are expensive, they offer considerable flexibility.
- *Cost*. Cost includes not just the interest charge, but also any fees (e.g. commitment fees) in order to have the facility available and money transmission costs. The cost of such fees needs to be balanced against the liquidity considerations of having the facilities available.
- *Diversification of sources*. It is better to have facilities from a number of sources rather than just one lender, provided that

the size of the borrower warrants this approach. This avoids the risk that the lender may either decide to reduce its exposure to the borrower or that capital becomes limited. In a practical sense, it will mean that the borrower is more widely known in the market and that some degree of competition on rates can be maintained. Diversification should apply not just to lenders, but also to markets – for example as between bank loans and securitised debt such as CP.

Overdrafts

One of the great advantages of the UK banking system is the availability of overdrafts. These are lines of credit made available on ordinary current accounts to companies at slightly more expensive rates than can be obtained through other markets, but which are repayable on demand. In practice, the demand feature is rarely used and some form of notice of withdrawal may be anticipated. Their great benefit is the flexibility that is afforded in the management of very short term liquidity.

Thus if the cash forecast shows a surplus for the current day of, say, £500000 but that there is a risk that the figure may vary by £250000, then the availability of an overdraft facility will allow the company to deposit £750000 but run the risk of an overdrawn balance of up to £500000. Given all possible outcomes, we can see that this is the preferred course of action. If we assume that overnight deposit rates are 10% and that the overdraft costs 12% and we look at the three cases of actual balances of £250000, £500000 and £750000, then the net interest receipts are as shown in Table 6.1. If we compare this with the alternative safe position of just depositing £250000 (assuming that we cannot go overdrawn), we see that we receive just £68.49 and with the possibility of £250000 or £500000 on a non-interest-bearing account.

Table 6.1   Use of overdrafts

	Actual balance		
	£250 000	£500 000	£750 000
Interest on deposit of £750 000	£205.48	£205.48	£205.48
Overdraft cost on balance	£164.38	£82.19	0
Net interest	£41.10	£123.29	£205.48

The potential loss of £27.39 if the balance turns out at the pessimistic end does not match the gain of £136.99 at the optimistic end. For major companies, where these decisions are taken over millions, the gains can be very significant. Furthermore, the process of cash forecasting should give an increasingly good feel for the margin of error, which may not be the same each day, and this will increase the benefit of the overdraft.

In spite of the flexibility of the overdraft, for companies experiencing liquidity problems the overdraft cannot be the sole source of finance because of its on-demand nature. There need to be other sources, but for companies where the actual level of cash is difficult to forecast, it is a particularly useful tool.

Overdrafts are available in countries other than the UK. However, care must be taken on the nature of the agreement with the bank. In some countries, it is illegal to overdraw an account without a formal arrangement. Charges may also vary between countries and banks. Some banks charge an annual arrangement fee, others charge on the basis of maintaining a compensating balance (which would rather obviate the point of an overdraft). Interest costs are additional to any arrangement fees.

- *Liquidity*. Care needs to be taken as these facilities can be repayable on demand – although they are not likely to be withdrawn without notice.

- *Flexibility*. Very flexible.
- *Cost*. More expensive than other forms of borrowing, but at the margin, the flexibility makes them cheaper than maintaining credit balances.

Committed and uncommitted facilities

Although loan facilities may be expressed to be available for a given period, drawings are frequently for shorter interest maturities and the selection of any particular interest period mirrors the decisions taken for deposits.

Of great significance for liquidity management is the difference between uncommitted and committed facilities. In the case of committed facilities, provided that the terms and conditions (which typically include financial covenants) of the loan agreement have been complied with, the lender is obliged to advance the funds. This is not the case for uncommitted facilities.

The balance of committed and uncommitted facilities depends very much on the financial standing of the borrower. For example, if the company is a small engineering company, then it will be preferable to ensure the availability of finance by negotiating a high level of committed facilities for the final £2 million or so. There is clearly not this requirement for large, financially stable corporations (although this may be so in a given overseas subsidiary where there is little liquidity in the domestic market). An alternative to a committed facility would be to have a loan that is fully drawn and to deposit temporarily any cash surpluses rather than repaying the loan.

Facilities may be negotiated with either a single bank or with a group of banks (known as a club or syndicate). It is beyond the scope of this book to describe funding management in a detailed manner. However, the basic principle of liquidity management is the availability of the borrowing facilities. Individual borrowings are made in the same manner as inter-bank deposits – that is they are for a set amount for a set period and at a set (fixed) rate. At the end of each borrowing, the borrowing may be *rolled over*, that is the principal amount does not need to be repaid (although the interest should usually be paid) and a new repayment date and interest rate are agreed.

Commercial paper

The main features of CP were described above and there are further restrictions in particular countries (especially in the sterling CP market, where the Bank of England has set limits on the size of company that can issue CP). In terms of the management of liquidity, CP may be regarded as a diversified source of uncommitted finance. It is useful to seek sources of funds outside the banking markets in order to leave credit room with the banks for other facilities (particularly as banks increasingly control their use of capital), but there is also the risk that the liquidity of the CP market will evaporate at precisely the point that funds are most needed. Therefore, the treasurer will need to be aware of other sources of finance for these eventualities.

The other great benefit of CP is that it tends to cost less than comparable bank loans. Commercial paper, in the form of negotiable bearer instruments, is issued through banks which act as dealers for the issuer and then place it with mainly non-bank investors. The dealers retain no exposure to the issuer once they have sold the paper. Typical maturities are 1, 2, 3 or 6 months. However, in the UK, CP may be issued for any period between 7 and 364 days and there are often shorter periods in order to suit an issuer's requirements.

The limits set on companies by the Bank of England for the sterling CP market are:

- companies must have net assets of over £25 million; and
- have shares or debt listed in London; or
- have shares or debt listed on an authorised exchange; or
- be incorporated in the UK.

Companies that are not themselves eligible can issue paper if it is guaranteed by a company which would be eligible in its own right, or by a bank. Commercial paper can also be issued by building societies and certain local authorities in England and Wales.

There are relatively modest costs associated with issuing CP by way of fees to the issuing and paying agent for handling the notes themselves. Additionally there will be printing costs for circulating mini-prospectuses to investors and also for the notes. The dealers themselves will usually earn their commission by making a profit between the buying and selling price ('making a turn') when the paper is issued.

A more substantial cost, both in time and money, will arise if it is decided to seek a credit rating (see above). Credit ratings are more common now and are obligatory in the domestic USCP market.

- *Liquidity*. This depends upon the state of the market, although it needs to be recognised that CP is an uncommitted arrangement.
- *Flexibility*. Subject to market conditions, the issuer can decide to issue in amounts and for dates that suit the issuer.
- *Cost*. Cheaper than borrowing directly from a bank.
- *Diversification*. CP offers an alternative to direct bank lending which may be constrained at various times.

Sterling bankers' acceptances

The consideration of cost is very important in looking at raising debt and as liquidity diminishes, the cost consequently rises owing both to scarcity of supply and to the increased risk of failure of the borrower.

For companies with sufficient trade related activity (as defined by the Bank of England), drawing bills of exchange on themselves and then having them accepted by an eligible bank can often be a cheaper way of raising debt than by borrowing directly from a bank. Acceptances were introduced in the section on bills of exchange on page 104. They operate in a similar way to direct bank facilities in that a company will arrange a facility with a bank to accept its bills. Such a facility may be either committed or uncommitted and the bank will charge an acceptance commission which is likely to be the same as the lending margin it would charge the same borrower. In effect, the difference between acceptances and direct bank loans is going to be one of cost – on some days acceptances may be cheaper.

Marginal sources of liquidity

When a company cannot borrow directly (or if it becomes prohibitively expensive), then the need to keep the company trading becomes paramount. At the extreme, this is real liquidity management in practice.

The control of working capital often becomes the issue. This may mean stretching payments to suppliers. Many companies will do this, but there is often a trade-off between prompt payment and receipt of discounts. At the other extreme, a steady increase in trade terms may lead to suppliers withdrawing their goods or, worse, to a general belief that the company is about to fail.

There will also be a reduction in costs and stocks. In the final extreme, cash will need to be raised by selling assets. For many companies the assets owned may be illiquid (such as land and buildings), but there may also be the option of factoring receivables. This will involve selling the right to receive the cash due from receivables in return for a discounted amount upfront. This can be an expensive method of raising cash, but may be the only solution available. In certain countries where the banking system is still based heavily on trade, this may indeed be the normal way of raising finance.

There are two basic types of factoring. The first is where the ownership of the receivable is passed to the factor, but the supplier continues to collect the amounts due. An alternative is invoice discounting whereby the factor also takes over the administration of chasing the payment. The choice involved will depend upon the needs of the borrower. Clearly, invoice discounting will be more expensive but will also relieve the borrower of administration costs.

Obtaining borrowing instruments

The critical difference in obtaining borrowing instruments, as compared to deposit instruments, is that the lender/investor will need to be willing to take a credit risk on the borrower/issuer. Consequently, banks will have a target market in mind and the chances are that the bank will try to market these instruments to the company, but at least the company should begin to understand what the bank is describing.

In any event, the prospective lender should always be able to present its business and its financial requirements in a clear manner. This is often the reason that otherwise sound businesses do not obtain the facilities that they need and could command.

7

Interest rate risk: definition and management

- An introduction to interest rate risk
- How to measure interest rate risk
- The objectives of interest rate management

In Chapter 5, the concept of interest rate risk was introduced. This is the exposure that the results of a business have to movements in interest rates. At its simplest, we can all understand that if borrowings are on a floating rate basis, then an increase in interest rates will reduce the profits of the business. There is also the concept of the opportunity cost of fixed interest rates: if a business places a deposit for a long period at fixed interest rates, then an increase in interest rates will represent a lost opportunity, especially if competitors are able to exploit this increase in a way that the business in question cannot. Finally, if an increase in interest rates means that customers are less inclined to buy the business's products or services, then there is an economic exposure to interest rates. For the purposes of this chapter, we will concentrate on the first example of interest rate risk.

Interest rate risk may be subdivided into:

- *Net interest risk.* This is the risk of loss as a result of parallel movements in the yield curve, i.e. that interest rates may move

115

either up or down. Net interest risk is the most common form of interest rate risk.

- *Spread risk.* This is the risk that loss may occur due to changes in the shape of the yield curve, i.e. the risk of mismatching assets and liabilities. So if a company has assets of 1 year funded by liabilities of 6 months, it is exposed to an increase in rates before the repricing of the liabilities at 6 months.
- *Volatility risk.* The current yield curve will assume a given level of volatility. This is most important for pricing hedging instruments. Volatility risk occurs when volatility changes as happened when sterling left the ERM in 1992.
- *Basis risk.* This is the risk of loss due to interest rates set on different bases, e.g. LIBOR compared with prime or UK base rate.

What is risk?

Risk is a concept that we encounter every day, not just in terms of interest rates. There is the risk that I might fall under a bus, but if I stay in bed that risk is zero. If I stand in the middle of the high street, the level of risk increases considerably. The same simple ideas apply to business risk. For example, there is a risk that a factory might burn down. I may not be able to avoid that risk, but I can limit the consequences by taking out insurance and I can reduce the risk by good risk management procedures. The premium for the insurance will be calculated by reference to past experience of my company and also to the industry in general. This will be calculated by using statistical methods and examining the probability of a particular event occurring. Thus risk in general may be considered as *any variation in expected outcome* – measured against an expected level.

Treasury departments manage primarily financial risk and the two major types of financial risk are currency risk and

116

interest rate risk. Currency risk is an entire subject in itself and is not discussed in this book. There are also a number of operational risks that apply to liquidity management. These include:

- *Counterparty risk.* The risk that a counterparty fails.
- *Settlement risk.* The risk that arises at the point of settlement of a transaction (e.g. on a swap).
- *Market risk.* The risk that an entire market moves against you or, indeed, fails.

Should interest rate risk be managed?

A question that often arises is whether or not risk should be managed. For publicly quoted companies, there is a strong argument that investors choose to invest in a company precisely because of the risks that arise in that company. Management needs to be clear about the *objectives* of any interest rate management and to communicate these clearly to investors.

For private companies and for sole traders, the question is often starker. How much risk can I afford to accept? It may be that interest rates are acceptable at current levels, but if they rise by five percentage points, then the increased costs will force the business into losses and possibly cash flow problems which could lead to insolvency. Risk might be considered in terms of current year profits. If investors are expecting a particular level of profits, then it might be better to fix interest rates at a level that would deliver those profits rather than leave open the possibility that they could go either up or down. Alternatively, risk might be considered in terms of the longer term financial structure. A business formed from a management buy-out is likely to have a high level of medium term debt and it would be more prudent to fix the interest rate on that debt to provide a secure planning base. But what should be done if there is strong expectation that rates will fall?

There is one school of thought that says that the market reflects all available information, so why should you have any better view than the market? Alternatively, there are different instruments available to manage interest rate risk in different ways. These are described in the next chapter.

In summary, the approach to managing risk is:

- first to identify it;
- next to measure it;
- then to set objectives for the management of the risk;
- then to manage it (which might include accepting the risk that exists);
- finally to monitor the management of the risk.

The measurement of interest rate risk

The components to take into account in measuring interest rate risk are the principal sum(s) involved and the possible range of future interest rates. The principal sums involved will be obtained from cash flow forecasts. However, the potential range of interest rates will be more difficult. If all rates are fixed then there is no problem, but life is rarely that simple. The starting-point will be the market's view as calculated from futures prices or longer term yield curves. An alternative source will be economic analysis which can be obtained either from specialist forecasting services or from major banks. Finally, there is also your own judgement.

A simple approach to measuring interest rate risk can be seen in the following example. Suppose a company is borrowing $10 million for 1 year at a current rate of 10%. The probabilities attached to potential future rates are given as:

50% that rates will stay at 10%
25% that rates will fall to 9%
25% that rates will rise to $10\frac{1}{2}$%

then the expected interest rate is $(10 \times 0.5) + (9 \times 0.25) + (10.5 \times 0.25) = 9.875\%$ and the interest cost for a year is expected to be $987 500. So any variation from this expected outcome represents one view of the risk involved.

An alternative approach is to apply sensitivity analysis. In the example above, we could have said that if rates rose to $10\frac{1}{2}$%, then there is a risk that costs would rise by $50 000. This particular risk could then be assessed either by looking at market expectations or by statistical analysis.

A further factor is volatility. The percentages set out above may have assumed the current degree of volatility. If the probability of rates changing increases and rates are said to be more volatile, then the overall risk will increase because there is a wider range of possible outcomes. So, if there is a risk that rates could rise to 12% (recall the volatility of sterling interest rates as sterling left EMU) then the exposure increases to $200 000.

The measurement of risk has become increasingly complicated and is now supported by a range of computer models, which measure volatility and standard deviation and then apply these measures to give a value. The most commonly used version of this is called value at risk (VAR). It is most appropriate for financial institutions but is beginning to be used by large companies. For many smaller businesses, however, these questions cloud the issue. A basic approach which identifies the range of possible outcomes and sets a comfort level to be managed towards will frequently be all that is required.

Modelling interest rate exposure

At the simplest level, the way to measure a company's interest rate risk is to take the business's current and forecast borrowings and deposits and to model the impact of a 1% movement in interest rates. Remember to apply the sensitivity test just to those cash flows that are exposed to floating interest rates. Those at fixed rates will not be affected.

Consider a company with a basic profit and loss account as follows:

	$m
Operating profit	40
Interest income	
Fixed rates (say 10%)	5
Variable rate (say 11%)	22
Interest expense	
Variable rate (say 12%)	(12)
Profit before tax	55

The net effect of a 1% increase in interest rates will now be to increase interest income by $2 million and to increase interest expense by $1 million, thus increasing profit by $1 million (assuming both deposit and borrowing rates move together).

For more complex situations this can be developed into maturity gap analysis.

Maturity gap analysis

The basic problem with simple sensitivity analysis is that it assumes that all borrowings and deposits are for one period only. As we have seen, interest rates are different for different periods. Thus, a company whose borrowings are all due to roll-over (or 'reprice') in 1 year's time as opposed to one whose borrowings roll over at a range of dates will have very different interest rate risks. If you now factor in a mixture of borrowings and deposits, you can see that this can lead to a complex range of questions.

Maturity gap analysis is one way of measuring interest rate risk in this situation. It is commonly used by banks and other financial institutions and also by corporates with a mixture of financial assets. For companies whose assets are mostly physical, rather than financial, the same approach can be used on a simplified basis. Its basic approach rests on the premise that if the same amount of assets and liabilities reprice at the same time then there is no net interest exposure. Other considerations are:

- if more assets (i.e. deposits) than liabilities (i.e. borrowings) reprice at a given date, then the company will gain from rising rates and lose from falling rates;
- conversely, if more liabilities than assets reprice at a given date, then the company will benefit from falling rates and lose from rising rates.

The procedure for using maturity gap analysis to measure interest rate risk is fairly simple:

1 Collect all the data on maturing loans and deposits. Take care to note that it is the date that they reprice (or roll over) that is important. So a 5-year loan with 6-month roll-overs reprices every 6 months.
2 Choose the gapping periods. These might be tomorrow, the next 7 days, 7–13 days, 13–28 days, 1–3 months, etc. The shorter the gaps, the more precise the answer but the model will also be more complex to run.

121

3 Associate plus signs with maturing or repricing assets (deposits) and minus signs with maturing, rolling over or repricing liabilities (loans).
4 Calculate the cumulative gap.

For example, suppose a business has the following loans and deposits maturing:

- an overnight deposit (i.e. now) of £5 million;
- a loan of £2 million which matures in 1 month;
- a deposit of £1 million which matures in 1 month;
- a loan of £5 million which matures in 2 months.

A simple gap analysis would be:

Period	Assets	Liabilities	Gap	Cumulative gap
0	5	0	5	5
1	1	2	−1	4
2	0	5	−5	−1

The risk could then be managed by creating liabilities in period 0 (overnight – which is not really practical) and then, depending what happened overnight, either by creating liabilities in period 1 or, if the funds were not required immediately, possibly by placing the maturing overnight deposit for 2 months thus reducing the risk at 1 month.

A practical alternative to the actual creation of further assets and liabilities (which is very costly in terms of bid–offer spread and use of the balance sheet) is to utilise the various off-balance sheet interest rate management instruments such as swaps, forward rate agreements, futures and interest rate options which are described in the next chapter.

If these instruments are used then care should be taken that they are included correctly in a maturity gap analysis as it is the *repricing* of an instrument which gives rise to the interest rate risk. So if a 3v6 FRA is purchased then that would reprice at 3 months (by the creation of a repriced asset) and then again at 6 months (as the repricing of a liability).

This approach ties in with the inclusion of future cash flows, so a maturity gap analysis should include all forecast needs. Thus if there were a £10 million borrowing for 3 months starting in 3 months' time to be hedged with a 3v6 FRA, then there is no net exposure as the gap analysis would show the liability in 3 months offset by the FRA and the repricing of the FRA in 6 months offset by the forecast cash flow to repay the borrowing. If, however, the loan is forecast to last for 4 months and there is still a 3v6 FRA, then there is a gap between months 6 and 7. This approach should be clearer after the next chapter when FRAs are described.

It should be remembered that maturity gap analysis is just a tool to aid decision-making. An analysis which shows consistently negative gaps shows an exposure to rising interest rates. The treasurer will have to form a view on whether s/he actually expects rates to rise and if so how to manage the risk. If an analysis shows wide fluctuations then it will be possible over time to even these out to avoid a exposure to a particular aspect of the short term yield curve (and, indeed, to the market generally).

Duration

Interest rate risk for longer term financial instruments is also measured by using duration and its related measures of modified duration and convexity. These more complex approaches are beyond the scope of this book both in terms of complexity and also because they apply more to longer term instruments such as bonds and gilts. Most non-financial businesses will have no need to use these techniques, but readers may be interested in a basic introduction that can be followed up in other books.

One of the weaknesses of maturity gap analysis arises from the length of a gap. For example, a 3-month 'gap' might involve assets at the beginning of the gap offset by liabilities at the end of the gap – so maturity gap analysis ignores the timing involved. Duration analysis attempts to avoid this by comparing the 'duration' of assets with the 'duration' of liabilities and is most often used with fixed income securities.

Technically, the duration of a security is the average of the maturity of all the cash flows involved, weighted by the present value of each cash flow. The precise formula is:

$$d = \frac{1}{p}\sum_t c_t t \left(1 + \frac{y}{f}\right)^{-ft}$$

where: d = MaCaulay duration; c_t = cash flow at time t years in the future; p = current price of the bond; y = yield to the maturity of the bond; and f = compounding frequency of yield to maturity.

If the objective of interest rate management is to avoid interest rate risk, then the duration of a portfolio would be zero. Assets have positive duration numbers and liabilities have negative duration numbers, so if an investor needs to protect against rising interest rates, negative duration should be maintained leaving the risk that interest rates fall.

Modified duration is a development that measures the interest rate sensitivity or the volatility in the price of an instrument for a small change in yield. Thus if a security has modified duration of 2, then for every basis point change in the yield, a price change of approximately 0.02% is expected.

Modified duration is calculated as:

$$\frac{Duration}{1 + \dfrac{r}{f}}$$

where r is the yield to maturity and f is the frequency of the coupon. Alternatively it can be stated as:

$$\frac{\Delta price}{\Delta yield}$$

Setting interest rate policy

Once interest rate risk has been identified and measured, it needs to be accepted or managed. However, such management can only occur if there is a clear policy setting out the board or owner's intentions. (This is indeed true for all treasury management where the policies as they apply not just to liquidity, but also to funding and currency management, should fit the overall business objectives.) This policy will set out how much liquidity the business needs to maintain and also how much risk it is prepared to accept.

For businesses operating within tight financial constraints and uncertain cash projections, the exposure to interest rate risk can prove the final straw. Therefore, the practical use of instruments that secure a future interest rate without the associated obligation to borrow or deposit is particularly helpful. But for many businesses, the most basic way to manage interest rate risk is to borrow on either a fixed or floating rate basis.

Therefore, it is normal to establish a proportion of borrowings (or deposits if there are especially large surpluses) to be set at fixed rates. For small companies, this proportion is likely to be fairly high given the need for predictability; but the ability to secure fixed rate debt is often limited by the unwillingness of lenders to advance funds for long periods or on a committed basis.

For very large companies, the proportion of fixed rate debt will form part of the basic decision on capital structure and will also be tied in to the level of gearing. However, the proportion of fixed rate debt is frequently associated with the income profile of a business. Thus, a leasing company with income streams linked to fixed interest rates will wish to reduce its exposure by having a high level of fixed rate debt.

In the end, the decision has to be a practical one based on the nature of the business, the perceived level of risk that the company wishes to accept and what can actually be transacted in the financial markets.

For large companies, the decision on the proportion of fixed rate debt is important. The two extreme positions are to have all the debt at floating rates or all the debt at fixed rates. Most businesses will determine a position somewhere in the middle. There has been the view that 50% fixed and 50% floating is the 'neutral' position but this may not be so. Each business will have a different sensitivity to interest rates depending, for example, on the level of non-income generating fixed assets compared with, say, a mortgage lender. The attitude of investors will also be important and so a business that seeks to set out a steady non-volatile growth track will have a higher, say 70%, proportion of its debt at fixed rates.

Having set a policy, the treasurer may then manage any exposure within that policy. This management may be 'static' in that any further risk is covered automatically or 'dynamic' whereby a view on rates is taken and timing decisions may be made. The next chapter looks at particular instruments used to manage interest rate risk, Chapter 9 examines liquidity management in practice and Chapter 10 looks at treasury organisation and the necessary controls.

8

Instruments for interest rate management

- An explanation of the instruments available to manage interest rates
- How to identify which instrument is suitable in a given situation

Before the 1980s the most obvious way to approach the issue of interest rate management was to borrow/invest at fixed or at variable rates with limited alternatives. However, since then derivative products have developed which permit the separation of interest rate management from the physical borrowing or investment. A 'derivative' is an instrument whose value and pricing depends upon or is derived from other underlying instruments. In the case of interest rate management this is most likely to be the secondary money markets and the capital markets which include government securities.

The instruments used to manage interest rates lead to one of two basic types of outcome:

- the securing of a known interest rate at some point in the future; or
- the securing of a known worst case for a future interest rate.

129

Both approaches provide the protection required. The second provides the opportunity to participate in beneficial movements in interest rates, but as a consequence may seem to be more expensive (the actual all-in cost can only be judged with the benefit of hindsight).

Forward forwards

In Chapter 5, the technique of disaggregating interest rates was explained. This resulted in establishing the market's view of interest rates for a given future period. This can be taken one step further to calculate a forward forward interest rate, that is, the rate at which a bank agrees to lend for a given period at some stage in the future.

Before the development of the instruments described later in this chapter, the rate for a loan for 3 months in 3 months' time was established by lending for 6 months, but re-depositing for the first 3 months. The calculations would be as explained for disaggregation, but the forward forward rate would be calculated by using the 6-month offer and 3-month bid. This clearly results in some fairly wide spreads and by the time the bank adds on the costs for using its balance sheet, the rates tend to become unattractive.

Forward rate agreements (FRAs)

The instrument that developed from the forward forward is the FRA, which allows the separation of the interest rate management from the actual borrowing or investment. An FRA is an agreement whereby two parties agree to fix the interest rate on a notional loan or deposit for a given future period commencing on a specified date and for a set amount. There is no requirement for the actual deposit or loan to be made with the bank or financial institution with which the FRA is undertaken. On maturity, if actual interest rates are different from the rate set under the FRA, then the effective interest differential (discounted for early receipt) passes between the two parties. Thus an FRA is a 'contract for difference', that is a contract where the principal amount underlying the transaction does not change hands, but where settlement is based on an ultimate difference.

A buyer of an FRA is the party wishing to protect itself against a future rise in interest rates, while the seller of the FRA wishes to protect itself against a future fall in interest rates. Therefore, a buyer of an FRA is a borrower and a seller of an FRA is a lender or investor.

The use of an FRA is probably best demonstrated by the following example.

It is currently 1 January and Company X has a borrowing requirement of $10 million for 6 months from 1 June. Interest rates are currently 8.43% for 6 months. Company X wishes to protect itself against a rise in interest rates and can achieve this by buying a 5v11 FRA. (Note that 5v11 means an FRA for a period which begins in 5 months' time and ends in 11 months' time.) On 1 January no money moves but Company X buys the FRA with an agreed rate of 8.62%. This represents the effective interest rate at which X will borrow for 6 months from 1 June.

At 1 June, interest rates have increased by 1% to 9.43% and therefore X is due to receive a settlement from the bank. The settlement is calculated as follows:

$$\frac{\left(0.0943-0.0862\right)\times10\,000\,000\times182/360}{1+\left(0.0943\times182/360\right)} = \$39\,085.62$$

131

This represents the interest differential between current 6-month rates (9.43%) and the agreed rate under the FRA (8.43%) on the principal sum ($10 million) for the period of the protection (6 months or, precisely, 182 days on the basis of a 360-day year), but discounted from 1 December to 1 June representing the convention that interest is normally paid at the end of the period.

We can confirm that the effective interest rate to X is in reality 8.62%.

On 1 June X receives	+39 086
On 1 June X borrows	+9 960 914
(i.e. 10 000 000 less the FRA receipt)	
On 1 December borrowing is repaid	−9 960 914
On 1 December interest at 9.43% paid	−474 876

Or, to put these together, in $:

1 June	+10 000 000
1 December	−10 435 790

$$\frac{10\,000\,000}{435\,790}\times100\times\frac{360}{182}=8.62\%\ \text{pa}$$

(Note that a 360-day year was used throughout as we were dealing with US dollars.)

The effect of using an FRA is to fix the interest rate, and therefore the treasurer needs to be relatively certain that the underlying cash flows will arise. In this sense, the use of FRAs provides a certain way of arranging fixed interest rates in the short to medium term.

FRAs are quoted for a range of future periods. Thus an FRA covering a period lasting 3 months and starting in 3 months' time is referred to as a 3v6 – that is, it covers the period between 3 months' time and 6 months' time.

FRAs are available in major currencies for periods going out beyond 2 years and are available for any amount agreed between the parties. In practice, however, better rates are achieved for larger sums, greater than £250000 or US$500000. FRAs are termed 'over-the-counter' instruments, that is they are not traded on an exchange but are discrete contracts agreed on a case by case basis. (Note, however, that their pricing is derived from exchange traded instruments.)

Financial futures

A financial futures contract is an agreement to buy or sell a standard quantity of a specific financial instrument (say, 3-month Eurodollar interest rates) at a predetermined future date, and at a price agreed between the parties through open outcry on the floor of an organised exchange (e.g. the International Money Market in Chicago or LIFFE in London).

The purchase or sale of a financial futures contract is a commitment to make or take delivery of a specific financial instrument at a predetermined date in the future, for which the price is established at the time of initial execution. For example, the purchase of a June 3-month Eurodollar contract commits the purchaser (if the contract is not sold in the market in the meantime) to make a deposit or to take a rate on a notional deposit of 1 million Eurodollars in June for 3 months at an agreed interest rate implicit in the price. (Note: the actual procedure depends upon the exchange being used, but in practice settlement is often avoided by buying or selling a matching contract.)

During the life of the futures contract, holders of open futures positions are able to identify related profitability. The standard nature of each futures contract makes such gains and losses easy to measure and monitor. Movements are tracked in terms of minimum price fluctuations known as 'ticks'. Each 'tick' is often (but not always) worth 1 basis point, i.e. 0.01% for interest rate futures such as short sterling or Eurodollar.

Typically, interest rate futures are quoted with a price as 100 minus the annual interest rate on the underlying instrument. Thus a price of 95.00 on the 3-month Eurodollar contract implies a rate of $100 - 95.00$ or 5.00% pa. Each tick on this contract is worth \$25 as the underlying contract operates in principal amounts of \$1000000 (check $1000000 \times 0.01\%$ $\times \frac{3}{12} = 25$). Similarly for 3-month sterling, where the contract standard amount is £500000, one tick is worth £12.50.

A member buying or selling a futures contract is required to lodge a deposit with the clearing house of the exchange called the initial or deposit margin. This is a fixed amount per contract and must be left in place as long as the position is held. In addition, daily variation margin is received from, or paid to, the clearing house as the position generates unrealised profits or losses as market prices move. In practice the actual obligation to deposit or lend is often satisfied by the sale or purchase of the appropriate contract at maturity. This approach means that investors in financial futures have a credit risk on the exchange, which in turn manages its risk by limiting the cash exposure. Any trader failing to meet margin calls could have the underlying contract closed out (by buying or selling) to remove the risk.

Financial futures have the severe limitations for many companies of complex administration and monitoring requirements. Furthermore, the standardised nature of the contracts means that they rarely match a particular requirement to borrow or deposit whether in amount or period. However, financial futures are very liquid instruments and sophisticated treasuries can use a mixture of the cash market and the futures market.

In practice, they achieve the same end result as FRAs, i.e. they fix a future interest rate, and indeed FRAs are in effect repackaged futures prepared by banks to suit their customers' precise requirements (in addition to the two-way trading in FRAs themselves). However, companies with regular hedging needs can, for example, hedge against rising interest rates by selling a future. Until the futures contract actually matures, the only cash flows are the initial and variation margin. On maturity the net position would be closed out by buying the contract. The net profit or loss on the futures contract would then be netted with the actual interest cost to give the net hedged position.

Both FRAs and futures are examples of hedging instruments that give a known future interest cost (or income). If situations change it is reasonably easy to reverse the position by creating an equal and opposite transaction. This may, however, give rise to either a profit or a loss. Thus it is important to have a clear forecast at the outset.

Swaps and longer term instruments

Interest rate (and currency) swaps have become a very familiar feature of the international capital markets since the mid-1980s. The basic feature of an interest rate swap is an agreement between two parties to exchange interest rates on two different bases on an agreed principal sum over a defined future period.

The most common example is the fixed floating swap. This is a method whereby one party will agree to make a series of floating rate interest payments based on a short term interest rate (say, 6-month LIBOR), and the other party will make a series of fixed rate payments based on a long term interest rate.

In practice, on each payment date the payments are netted against each other so that only the party owing the greater amount makes the net payment. In a swap involving only one currency, no principal is exchanged.

The great benefit of swaps for many small and medium-sized companies has been the ability to raise what is, in effect, fixed rate debt at times when the traditional fixed rate debt markets could not be accessed by companies of their size. More widely, all companies can change the interest profile of their liabilities without needing to raise fresh debt.

Swaps are more appropriate for longer term positions. In the short term FRAs are an equivalent product. In fact, interest rate swaps may be regarded almost as a series of FRAs.

Options

All the instruments discussed so far involve fixing the rate for future obligations. These work well in an environment where future cash flows are predictable or where there are clear obligations. However, what can a company do when an increase in interest rates would place undue pressure on a business and where it is unclear whether certain cash flows will arise in any event? These situations occur all the time, for example when a company is considering bidding for another company and has to plan the interest costs which might arise if the bid does not succeed.

The use of interest rate options provides a solution to deal with these situations. An option contract gives the purchaser the right, but not the obligation, to lock in a rate in the relevant underlying financial instrument, at a predetermined price, at a time in the future. In return for this right the purchaser pays a premium to the seller (also known as the writer) of the option.

Options are an increasingly familiar feature and occur in everyday life. For an example, if I pay a non-refundable deposit of £100 to buy a car, but if I have to decide in the next 10 days whether or not actually to buy the car, then I have bought a 10-day call option on that car and the option premium is £100.

An option that gives the holder the right to buy an underlying asset (e.g. the car, but perhaps a financial future) is called a 'call option'. An option that gives the holder the right to sell (and thus force someone else to buy) is called a 'put option'.

Options may be traded on an exchange or over-the-counter (for most companies over-the-counter is more practical). Almost all exchange traded options are American style (i.e. they can be exercised at any time); over-the-counter may be either American or European style (i.e. exercisable only at maturity), but are often European.

In addition to the premium paid by the purchaser of the option, the other significant features to be agreed are:

1 *Amount.* How much of the underlying financial instrument is involved.
2 *Strike price.* The strike price is the interest rate that the holder of the option has the right to receive:
   (a) at the money – strike price equal to current market forward rates;
   (b) in the money – strike price more advantageous to buyer than current market rates (higher premium);
   (c) out of the money – strike price less favourable to buyer than current market rates (lower premium).
3 *Type of option.* There are broadly two types of option: American-style options, which can be exercised at any time up to the expiry date or European-style options which can only be exercised on fixed dates.

An important feature of options is to ensure that the hedge that is being required is actually achieved by the transaction intended. Thus companies are only likely to buy call or put options. Companies wishing to hedge against rising interest rates are likely to buy a call option; those wishing to hedge against falling rates will buy a put option. They are most unlikely to want to *sell* either type of option. This is because all the seller receives is the option premium. After a certain point the seller of the option is exposed to unlimited losses (conversely the holder or purchaser of the option is exposed to unlimited gain). In this manner, options are highly geared instruments and realistically only seasoned professionals sell them. Figures 8.1 and 8.2 show the profit/loss position from the viewpoint of a purchaser and seller of a call option.

It can be seen from Figure 8.1 that the all-in hedged cost to the purchaser of an option is the strike rate *plus* the option premium *if the option is exercised.* At expiry of the option if the option is still out of the money (that is, market rates are lower than the strike rate in the case of a call option) then the option will be allowed to lapse and the all-in rate will be the actual market rate plus the option premium.

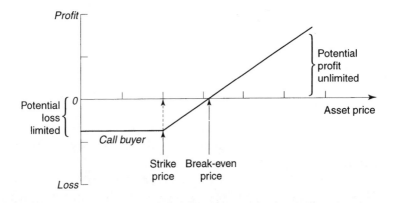

8.1 Buy a call option.

138

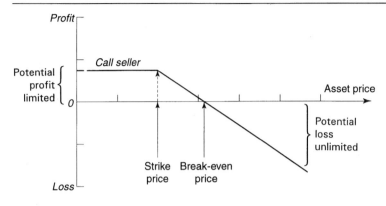

8.2 Sell a call option.

The pricing of options is a complicated subject which commands a book in itself. The principal components of pricing are the time involved and the intrinsic value (that is, the difference between the current market price of the underlying instrument and the strike price). An option only has intrinsic value once the market price is greater than the strike price. Thus if an option is not in the money then its value is all time value. The components that make up the valuation of an option are the riskless rate of interest, the time involved and most importantly the volatility of the returns on the underlying instrument, measured as the standard deviation. Many companies will not have access to the models necessary to value options; therefore the best approach is to regard the option as insurance and to compare the cost with other alternatives available. Competing market quotations can be obtained to establish the true value, recalling that the further out of the money an option is, the cheaper it will be in terms of initial premium, given the lower likelihood that it will be exercised. Figure 8.3 shows the time value and intrinsic value associated with a call option.

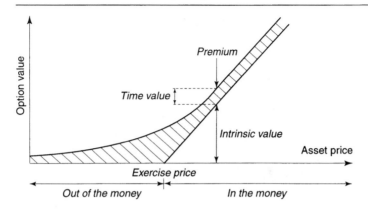

8.3 Time value and a call option.

Example

If we return to the example used to explain FRAs on p 131, another solution might have been to hedge the borrowing requirement by an option. In this case the company would have bought a call option on 6-month Eurodollar LIBOR. If the strike price were, say, 8.5% with a premium of 0.175% pa, then the calculation would have been as follows.

Premium: $10\,000\,000 \times 0.00175 \times 151/360 = \$7340.27$

By 1 June, interest rates are higher than the strike price. Therefore, it is profitable to exercise the option and to borrow at 8.5%. If we ignore the funding costs of the option premium, total costs are:

$$10\,000\,000 \times 0.085 \times 182/360 = \$429\,722.22 + \$7340.27$$
$$= \$437\,062.49$$

to give an effective interest rate of 8.645% pa compared with the cost of 8.62% pa using FRAs.

All other things being equal, options should be expected to be more expensive than FRAs or futures because of the additional flexibility. Many companies find the up-front premia unacceptable particularly in an environment of cost-cutting. However, if this is compared to general insurance and placed in the context of overall interest costs, a reasonable strategy can be developed. The increasing flexibility associated with options means that in times of greater volatility they represent a good, cost effective solution.

In an environment when future cash flows are uncertain and a company wishes both to limit its interest rate exposure and to fix the cash outlay if funds do not arise, then options provide a relatively straightforward peace-of-mind solution.

Caps, floors and collars

While swaps fix interest rates for future dates, it is also possible to limit interest cost or interest income by using caps and floors respectively. These are packaged interest rate option products.

In the case of a cap, in return for a premium, a bank will agree to pay a company the interest differential based on a set principal if a given interest rate (say 6-month LIBOR) is above an agreed fixed rate (e.g. 14%) on certain fixed dates. Conversely, a floor operates below a set rate and therefore is used to protect interest income.

In order to minimise the premia required for floors and caps a company might agree to limit any benefit received from falling interest rates (if using a cap) by paying to the bank the interest differential if rates fall below a set level (e.g. 12%). Thus, the company could be assured that its interest cost would fall between the two levels (e.g. 12 and 14%). This is known as a collar. Caps, floors and collars can be shown diagrammatically as in Figure 8.4.

Caps, floors and collars are not restricted just to the medium and long term; they can be used for shorter periods, although this is not their normal use. A collar over 6 months may be regarded as a low cost option (see below), while certain UK clearing banks are attempting to introduce base rate caps and base rate FRAs (i.e. those that limit the cost of base rates) for their smaller corporate customers.

Clearly, the cost of the cap, floor or collar increases the overall cost of borrowing for the period when no payment is received and in the case of a collar this can be seen diagrammatically as in Figure 8.5.

Two simple examples are considered below.

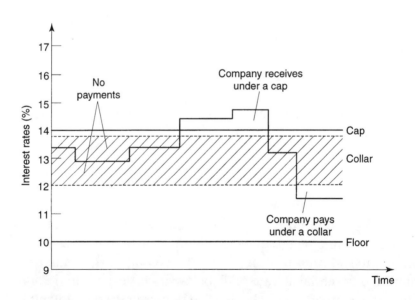

8.4 Caps, floors and collars.

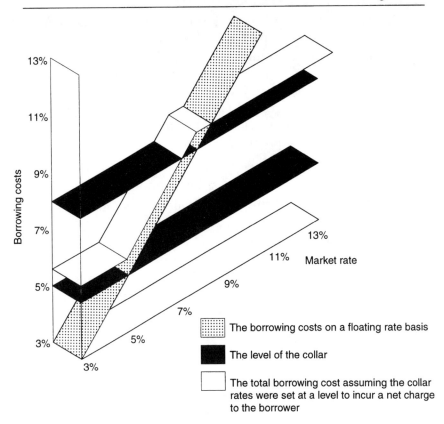

8.5 Interest rate collar.

Company D

This has a borrowing programme of $100 million which is currently all based on floating rates. The loans are from a variety of banks and the programme is expected to last 5 years. Roll-overs are due in 3 months' time.

The central questions here are: how much fixed rate debt does the company want and what is its current view of interest rates?

1 If it believes that rates might rise, it could decide to take out an interest rate swap on part of its debt (say, 50%).
2 If it believes that rates might rise in the short term, but then fall again, it could take out FRAs or options in the short term or buy a swap for less than 5 years.
3 If it believes that rates will fall, it could leave all its debt on a floating basis but protect itself by buying a cap at a highish rate for a relatively low premium.

These are not the only strategies, but I hope that they begin to show the number of choices available. Note also that the view on interest rates is central to the strategy to be adopted. Of course, an overriding policy decision might be taken to have a certain proportion of debt at fixed rates, in which case there may be an issue of tactical timing on when to fix. In any event, once a strategy has been adopted, that is not the end of it. Conditions change and therefore there needs to be a constant review to ensure that overall objectives continue to be met.

Company E

This is a small business trading near the limits of its borrowing facilities, and it has monthly cash flow difficulties. It is exposed to a potential trading downturn in a few months' time which would be made worse by an increase in interest rates.

In this case, the clear requirement is to limit the interest cost. A small company may be unable to obtain options, but more importantly unable to pay the premia in the short term. Therefore, the use of FRAs if the bank will agree to these would be desirable or, failing that, just fixed rate debt.

The real problem in this type of situation is that, no matter what the theoretical solution, the practical problems of obtaining the necessary instrument or credit approval will limit room for manoeuvre.

A note on taxation

As with all treasury matters, the taxation consequences need to be considered carefully. Not only do local taxation regimes dictate the particular company in the group to be used to ensure deduction for payments made, but the after-tax interest cost must be considered.

In particular, although payments under swaps, FRAs and options may attract a deduction for taxation, the effective cost needs to recognise that there may be a timing mismatch between allowance for these payments and for interest (which can be on a paid basis). In the UK, the current taxation regime has moved to align the taxation treatment to provide a better hedge. However, these consequences can cloud the basic issue of whether or not to hedge for many smaller companies, which need to concentrate on both the liquidity available and the desired end result.

9

Liquidity management in practice

- Putting the theory into practice
- Some simple case studies

The principal objective of liquidity management is always to maintain liquidity so that a company or organisation (or for that matter an individual) can continue to meet its commercial objectives. But there is also the task of managing the liquidity in an optimal way in the best interests of the organisation.

The general approach to liquidity management in practice has already been set out as safety, liquidity and profitability, to which can now be added the management of risk. By putting all these together we can now address the following practical questions: how much, for how long, what instrument and for what return? But liquidity management cannot be reduced to one decision, say, to invest in a CD for 3 months at 10% and to leave it at that. The dynamics of both the market-place and the underlying business mean that decisions need to be kept under active review to ensure that overall objectives (and especially the principal objective of maintaining liquidity) continue to be met.

147

The general approach

In earlier chapters the various concepts and tools used in liquidity management have been described. We can now put these together to see how decisions might operate in relatively complicated situations.

The starting-point is to develop a cash forecast for a given future period and then look at it critically in the context of the business. This will give certain alternatives for funding or depositing, in terms both of amount and period. Interest periods can then be selected against a view of interest rates, leading to a selection of market and instrument. If need be, future interest rates can be hedged to deal with uncertainty (either against movement in rates or in cash flow). The resulting decision is then kept under review and the process repeated each time there is a change in circumstances. The flow chart in Figure 9.1 sets out the process in a simplified way.

In order to demonstrate the process in practice, let us consider some cases and look at the alternative decisions that can be taken at each stage.

Case studies

Seasonal PLC

Seasonal PLC is a retailer where sales are made for cash and arise in two main selling seasons. Goods are purchased up to 3 months ahead of sale, but orders are placed many months before this and there is limited opportunity to cancel orders once placed. Costs are predictable and not linked to the level of sales.

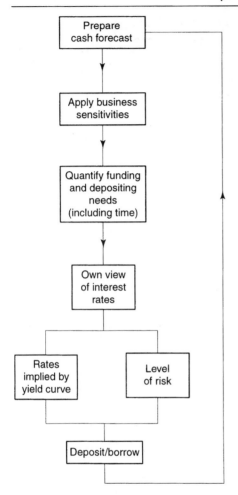

9.1 The process of liquidity management.

The cash forecast (prepared on a receipts and payments basis) at the beginning of the year was as shown in Table 9.1. The opening balance at the beginning of January was £40 million borrowed. (Note: in order to simplify the example, capital expenditure and interest have been omitted and it may be assumed that separate funding will be available to manage these exposures.)

149

Table 9.1 Seasonal PLC: cash forecasts ($£$ million)

	J	*F*	*M*	*A*	*M*	*J*	*J*	*A*	*S*	*O*	*N*	*D*
Sales	80	30	32	40	40	60	35	30	45	74	100	120
Purchases	5	15	40	30	30	15	20	50	80	70	20	10
Tax			25									
Dividends				20				5				
Costs	5	5	22	5	5	22	5	10	22	10	5	22

These forecasts give total cash forecasts of:

(40) 30 40 (15) (30) (25) (2) 8 (22) (84) (90) (15) 73

It is often helpful to represent these graphically, as in Figure 9.2. This highlights the cash swings in the year and shows a period of heavy borrowing starting in August and a period of modest surplus early in the year and in December.

With this information, we can begin to address two key questions:

1 What level of borrowing facilities should be available?
2 How long should each borrowing be and what do we do about interest rate risk?

First, we need to consider the cash forecast carefully. Assume that sufficient care has been taken in its preparation (although in practice this should not always be assumed). The following points need to be noted. It is not clear whether sales and purchases move evenly with each other in a month. Given the evidence that purchases are bought well in advance of sales, it may be possible that during September and October, in particular, the peak borrowing requirement may exceed the month-end position and thus approach $£150$ million.

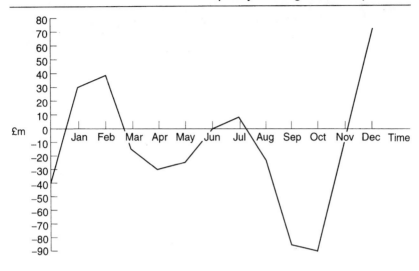

9.2 Seasonal PLC: total cash forecasts.

Next, it is necessary to look at the sensitivity of the cash forecast. If sales turn out to be lower than forecast, then the usual response will be to reduce the intake of stock to match the lower sales level. If the sales downturn becomes apparent only during September, there may be little that can be done about orders for stock already placed. Thus the effect of a 15% reduction in sales forecast (not so unusual in the recession in the UK of 1989–91) would be to increase the absolute year-end borrowings by £50 million. The exact phasing of this would also depend on whether there was any delay in the actual timing of spending as Christmas approached. In any event, there would be a higher level of borrowing and for longer than anticipated. The increase in borrowings might be reduced gradually by management action during the following months.

If, however, sales turn out to be better than forecast, the effects would be cash receipts earlier than forecast, but the need to pay more quickly for further stock (always assuming

Table 9.2 Seasonal PLC: current interest rates

Months	%
1	$10\frac{1}{2} - \frac{1}{4}$
2	$10\frac{1}{2} - \frac{1}{4}$
3	$10\frac{3}{4} - \frac{1}{2}$
6	$10\frac{3}{4} - \frac{1}{2}$
9	$10\frac{7}{8} - \frac{5}{8}$
12	$10\frac{3}{4} - \frac{1}{2}$

that it would be available). The effect of this on the absolute level of borrowings, on the same basis that the sales variation becomes clear in September, is likely to be neutral, with the likelihood of a reduction by perhaps £25 million during September and October and from December onwards.

The effect of all these points is that there needs to be approaching £200 million of facilities available to be safe. The majority of these will not be needed until September and should be repaid by the end of the year. Since this pattern clearly recurs each year, it would be sensible to have at least £50 million available by way of a committed facility for, say, 5 years, which can also be drawn and repaid at will. In order to arrange the remaining facilities, bankers will need a very clear view that these are the ongoing seasonal requirements of the business so that they will not be surprised at the level of borrowings later in the year. The level of committed facilities will depend upon the track record and current profitability of Seasonal. Thus if trading is well established, then a more relaxed view can be taken.

The second question dealt with periods of borrowing and interest rate risk. Current interest rates are shown in Table 9.2.

It can be seen from the general shape of the yield curve and by disaggregating that the market expects interest rates to fall gently over the coming year. However, there is considerable room for change and the trend is by no means clear. In particular, the rates for certain interest periods may be driven by the liquidity in the market for that period (especially for unusual periods such as 9 months).

If we look back at Figure 9.2, there are a number of funding alternatives. These include:

1 Borrowing or depositing for the longest period suitable. So, for example, borrowing £25 million for 3 months at the end of August and incrementally thereafter.
2 Borrowing £25 million in April for around 8 months and depositing any short term surpluses in the meantime.

In fact, there are a large number of complex options that arise. However, it is often better to keep it simple by maintaining a broad overview. The essential feature about this business is the very steep exposure to the cost of borrowing in the second half of the year.

First, it is helpful to calculate the market's expectation of borrowing rates at the end of the year by disaggregating the 3-month rate in 9 months' time. This is calculated as:

$$\left(1+i_m\right) = \frac{1.1075}{\left(1+0.10875\times\dfrac{9}{12}\right)}$$

$$= 1.02398$$

i.e. the 3-month rate in 9 months' time is expected to be of the order of 9.6% (2.398×4). This is also likely to be reflected in the current 9v12 FRA rate.

Compared to current rates, this fall would be beneficial, but Seasonal PLC would need to set its own view of rates against this. Every 1% movement in rates over the period August–November would mean around £132 500 in interest cost. While this is a large amount, it is not going to be critical to the future existence of the company. However, there is a clear opportunity to manage the future interest cost.

Therefore, if FRAs (either 8v11 or 9v12, i.e. for periods of 3 months to begin in either 8 or 9 months' time and to end in 11 or 12 months' time) can be bought at under 10%, it might be prudent to do so unless there is a very strong view that rates might fall further. If there is that belief, then protection could be obtained by purchasing 3-month interest rate options to expire in 8 or 9 months' time.

The essential feature from this point is to keep the situation under review. Cash forecasts will continue to be prepared and these should show any significant variance from expectations. In particular, a deterioration in sales will allow the following action:

- early revision of purchases;
- further protection against rising rates;
- if need be, the negotiation of further facilities.

In effect, it is likely that the first sign of trouble will be identified in the treasury department and it will require some diplomacy to persuade other colleagues of the need for action.

We have met Seasonal PLC before, when considering how to look at variations in forecast in Chapter 3. The original forecast for the months of October to December was:

(90)   (15)   73

but turned out to be:

(110)   (50)   20

In practice, as October approached, better information would have shown the need to borrow more and for longer, but with the same result of cash positive by the end of the year. On the basis that the facilities had been arranged, Seasonal PLC would have the alternatives of borrowing for 1, 2 or 3 months depending on its view of the interest rates available at the time. Again, in practice, unless the view on rates was held very strongly, two reasonable approaches would have been either to borrow for the longest period for which funds were expected to be available or to average over time by choosing a mixture of the periods available.

So, overall, Seasonal PLC could manage all the information available to it: the cash flows as they changed, the interest rates currently obtainable and its own expectations of them, and also the hedging instruments and borrowing facilities open to it, to ensure that the necessary liquidity was both available and managed in the most efficient manner.

International Cruises Inc

This company operates in two divisions. The larger one is the shipping division which is capital-intensive and is highly geared by loans which are secured on the ships owned by the division (rather like mortgaging houses). The shipping division receives its income from shipping cargo, but also from trading in the value of its ships, which has been rising due to under-supply.

The other part of the business is the tourism division which generates strong cash flow by selling holidays and taking deposits in the early part of the year, but only paying suppliers (airlines, hoteliers) later in the year. This division is profitable.

In addition to the loans secured on the ships, the group is funded by overdrafts and unsecured loans totalling $50 million. These facilities are on demand and are reviewed each October after the main season. It is now December and the facilities are in place (albeit on an on-demand basis) for the coming months. As is usual, it is planned to use the cash flow from the tourism division to support the activities of the shipping division.

Cash forecasts for the coming months are as shown in Table 9.3. It is clear that the company can only just live within its facilities and is dependent on the early cash receipt from a ship sale and the continuing cash flow from the tourism division. It is also clear that, during this part of the year, the main shipping activity is a cash drain (indeed it is only likely to break even in the early part of the year). The continuing drain in cash terms of the shipping division is being financed by the tourism division and also by ship trading (although $10 million will be required to meet the first instalment of a new ship during April).

In this environment, many of the more normal issues in liquidity management, such as choice of interest period, become secondary to ensuring continuing cash flow. The ship loans will be at fixed interest rates, therefore those cash flows are predictable, but the company is heavily exposed to both an increase in interest rates and to a downturn in business. In situations where the central issue is going to be a lack of

Table 9.3 International Cruises Inc: cash forecasts ($ million)

	Dec	Jan	Feb	Mar	April	May
Opening position	(30)					
Tourism	5	5	10	10	15	20
Shipping	(8)	(8)	(18)	(18)	(16)	(3)
Ship trading	–	25	–	–	–	–
Interest	(2)	23	(2)	(2)	(12)	(2)
Closing position	(35)	(15)	(25)	(35)	(48)	(33)
Agreed facilities	(50)	(50)	(50)	(50)	(50)	(50)

liquidity and where there is an exposure to rising interest rates, the best course of action would be to draw loans for the longest period possible. (Note: the treasurer and relevant directors should always be aware of the ethical and legal considerations of drawing loans for long periods – or, indeed, any period – if they have misled bankers as to the true position or if there is a risk of trading while insolvent. There is a fine line between ethical actions and the risk of making a business needlessly bankrupt.) This action removes the risk that an already difficult situation might be worsened by an additional pressure.

But in this case, the chief financial officer (CFO), treasurer or other manager responsible for the liquidity of the group will need to anticipate what else could be done. In practice, the banks would not withdraw their facilities as that act alone would force the business to cease trading – their repayment would come from normal receipts. However, it is equally unlikely that further facilities are going to be available without good reason. In this context, the underlying profitability and future viability of the group become critical.

There are two significant sensitivities here:

1 The receipt of $25 million from ship trading.
2 The certainty of receipts from tourism.

If the $25 million is delayed for, say, 3 months (and this is entirely possible – delay in negotiations, lack of finance for the purchaser, collapse in ship values, etc), then the group will be at the limit of its facilities in February and will exceed them from March onwards. Any room that might be available in February would be removed if there were the slightest slippage in tourism receipts. Action therefore needs to be taken now to arrange further finance. Management of working capital should already be tight, involving stretching payables and attempting to accelerate receivables.

Otherwise, there are four ways to improve the cash position:

1 Raise equity.
2 Negotiate further debt.
3 Sell assets.
4 Cancel capital expenditure.

In a situation where the position is marginal, all four should be attempted simultaneously. The sale of assets may take a long time (and a major asset is the tourism division), but there could be a good case for sales at bargain prices, although this can give too clear a message to the outside world. If there is no cash available, then capital expenditure cannot be paid for, but contingency plans need to be prepared to handle the $10 million payment due in April. This will involve anticipating the supplier's reaction to delaying delivery.

However, the major efforts will need to be directed at raising either equity or debt. Both have the problem of the viability of the business, in particular the cash outflow of the shipping division. Investors and lenders will need a clear statement of the management action to be taken to improve the position. This plan needs to be available or else funds are highly unlikely to be obtained. Indeed, a reporting accountants' report may be required. All this will take time which means that efforts need to be concentrated in three areas:

1 Ensuring the earliest receipt of $25 million.
2 Managing the continuing business.
3 Preparing action plans and presentations.

Success will depend upon the quality of the management and the credibility of their plans. If there has been regular and clear communication throughout, then it is more likely that they will succeed. At one level further on, control may be removed from them by either lenders or shareholders if they are not success-ful. In the final analysis, lenders and shareholders can decide that enough is enough and the group may fold.

What is clear is that a senior member of management must always be aware of the key factors that ensure continuing liquidity and maintain the external relationships with those who provide it.

D and L Engineering

This is a small business with one employee other than the owner, serving the offshore oil industry and local agricultural community in north-east Scotland. It was established with the proprietor's capital of £20000 and bank loans and overdraft of the same amount together with a regional interest-free loan to purchase machines of £10000 from the local development agency. This is to be repaid in monthly instalments starting in 18 months.

The first 6 months of the business were taken up with setting up the workshop and developing the necessary business con-tacts. A number of regular orders were obtained and the major customers accounted for the following proportions of the work: A 60%; B 20%; C 5%. The balance of orders were from local farmers, but an increasing reputation for prompt and high quality work means that this area is growing. There is little time to seek new contracts as existing customers more than occupy current capacity, even though this might be desirable to diver-sify the customer base.

The first full year's turnover was £80000 and there was a healthy profit of £25000. Drawings had not been high, yet the overdraft limit of £10000 was often close to being exceeded. There was a need to expand the business by buying new machines costing £15000 and by employing another engineer in order to take some pressure off the existing staff. This would leave seven machines between the three of them.

A closer examination of the past 3 months' figures is given in Table 9.4. In order to buy the new machine, the owner decided to approach his bank for a further loan. The initial reaction from the bank was that it wished to continue to support this business but that it would need clear projections for the coming year and also seek a steady reduction of the overdraft.

This prompted a detailed analysis of the current position in order to establish the next few months. In particular, the working capital position needed examination. In order to support him, the owner employed an accountant for a few hours to carry out the analysis.

On the assumption that the proportions of work carried out for A and B were correct, then total receipts in the last 3 months from A should have been around £12000 and from B around £4000. However, the actual figures were £6900 and £1000 respectively. Clearly, both these areas warranted further examination.

A detailed analysis revealed:

• A took 30 days' credit provided that the invoices were submitted by the end of the month; otherwise they would have to wait until the end of the following month.

Table 9.4 D and L Engineering: past 3 months' figures

	Month		
	1	*2*	*3*
Sales	6500	6250	7150
Receipts from A	3000	2900	1000
Receipts from B		1000	
New machines	2500		

- The owner had failed to submit invoices totalling £5000 to A due to pressure of work.
- B took erratic periods of credit, but there were £3000 of invoices more than 45 days past due.
- A complete analysis of all sales and invoices showed that there were more than £10000 of invoices either not submitted or overdue (i.e. over 30 days).

Thus, £10000 could be raised from sorting out the debtor position alone. This would ensure the complete removal of the overdraft. A further analysis showed that the current level of profitability would pay for the machine in a little over 5 months within the current overdraft.

There also needed to be an analysis of the other components of working capital. D and L held little stock, which tended only to be bought in as needed; therefore this was unlikely to be a problem. However, D and L had always prided itself on paying its bills on time. This meant in practice that bills were paid weekly. If D and L moved on to taking 21 days' credit, this would release a further £1500 into the business.

The simple pressures of day-to-day business had meant that a lack of control could have led to unnecessary financial pressures. The introduction of a monthly financial review would allow adequate control of working capital as well as a better analysis of the business, including costing of individual jobs and identification of the most profitable business.

Megacorp

This is a diversified multinational corporation based in the USA with a market capitalisation of $5 billion. It is about to launch a bid for Target PLC for £2.5 billion. The acquisition will be financed by debt denominated in sterling, which will be repaid by a mixture of asset disposals and operating cash flow. It has been decided to manage the currency exposure from the potential acquisition by borrowing in sterling from a banking syndicate. There is the possibility of raising fresh equity if need be.

There are a number of liquidity management issues which arise from this acquisition:

1 Megacorp is exposed to rising sterling interest rates. It will not wish to draw down the loans before it actually has to pay for Target. Indeed the acquisition may not proceed. In this case, it could protect itself against this risk by taking out options on sterling interest rates. Further, because the size of the acquisition is so large, it may also wish to purchase 'swaptions' (options on swaps) so that it can decide to fix a large element of the potential sterling debt.

2 If the acquisition proceeds, it will want to be able to use any free cash within Target as well as its operating cash flow. Therefore, it must have ready systems to allow it to:
    (a) obtain reliable cash forecasts promptly after acquisition;
    (b) net surplus cash within Target against borrowings within the rest of Megacorp;
    (c) impose daily cash reporting of balances within Target;
    (d) establish intra-group payment systems in order to limit bank charges;
    (e) impose deposit policies and limits;
    (f) renegotiate borrowing facilities;
    (g) identify and sell any peripheral assets in Target.

In reality, these are the same controls and systems that any business of whatever size would need, but without the day-to-day operational controls, which a company the size of Target should have in any case. The basic principles would remain the same, even though the companies operate in different countries. Local money transmission rules and banking systems and instruments may differ, but the basic issues of:

162

- cash flow information;
- analysing that information;
- selecting appropriate instruments;
- managing interest periods and risk;

will be the same the whole world over. In the final analysis, ensuring the availability of cash to meet liabilities will be the first objective of both liquidity and treasury management.

Conclusion

Hopefully these case studies show that, no matter the scale of the business, liquidity needs to be addressed. Small companies may not need complex instruments, but cash forecasting, the availability of liquidity and depositing are core activities.

Figure 9.1 can be used as a template for all businesses, but with different emphases.

10

Organising liquidity management

- Establishing policies
- Setting authorities for the organisation of liquidity management
- Ensuring appropriate controls

For many small businesses not all the techniques described in this book will be applicable, and similarly some of the functions may well be carried out as part of the duties of the bookkeeper or accountant. However, the basic principles can be followed by businesses of whatever size.

For larger companies, and certainly for large multinational groups, the business of liquidity management normally forms part of the treasury department which ought to have suitably experienced and qualified staff. For all companies there will need to be an agreement on how the staff are to be monitored and evaluated and also how much delegated decision-taking will take place. While the day-to-day business of money transmission and managing short term depositing and borrowing should be capable of being left in the hands of operational staff, policy decisions about deposit limits and interest rate policy need to be reviewed and approved by at least the finance director and, ideally, by a suitable board subcommittee.

These instructions should set out the limits within which specified members of staff may operate and how exceptions are to be approved. The initial judgement by the board (or whoever that judgement is delegated to) needs to be taken after careful consideration of the risks involved. After all, if the policy is complied with and something goes wrong, the board will need to recognise its own involvement. (Even if the policy has not been complied with, then there are questions about control.) Typically, the initial proposal might be made by the treasurer, so that is where the greatest responsibility lies.

However, no treasury management policy should exist without a clear understanding of how treasury fits in with the overall strategic objectives of the group. This is quite apart from more detailed policies setting out how the overall policy is to be operated.

Treasury policy in context

Overall treasury policy will establish major financial parameters such as gearing level, distribution policy, interest cover and the level of risk to be accepted. Within that context, liquidity policies should establish the following:

- level of borrowing facilities to be maintained;
- amount of cash to be kept in liquid instruments;
- maximum period for investment;
- instruments to be used for investment;
- proportion of fixed/floating rate debt;
- instruments to be used for short term interest rate management;

and, very importantly,

- counterparty limits for banks and corporates with clear methods of calculating risk for derivatives and foreign exchange contracts.

A typical initial approval might include the following aspects.

Deposit policy

Deposits may only be placed with the following institutions and totals outstanding with each may not exceed the amount specified:

- £20 million: A, B, C, D.
- £10 million: E, F, G, H.
- £5 million: I, J.
- £1 million: K, L, M, N, P, R, S, T.

Additionally, commercial paper may be purchased for periods of up to 1 month with a limit of £5 million for any one group of companies and with a maximum maturity of 1 month provided that the issuer (or guarantor) has a rating of at least A1, P1.

Deposits in excess of 6 months must be approved by the finance director and in excess of 1 year by the treasury committee.

Interest rate policy

- It is the general policy that x% of borrowings greater than 1 year should be at fixed interest rates.
- Interest rate options which do not reflect an underlying borrowing or deposit requirement must not be bought.

167

- Interest rate options must not be sold (i.e. written).
- Detailed management of interest rate risk less than 1 year is delegated to the treasury committee.

(Note: the policy would also extend to more detailed funding management and also to detailed policy on currency management.)

Money transmission policy

In addition, there might be more detailed policies covering money transmission, which would include:

- methods of transmission;
- banks to be used;
- authorised signatories;
- dual controls for electronic transmissions;
- agreed cost structures.

Putting liquidity into practice

References are made above to a treasury committee. It is a matter of individual judgement as to how much policy should be reserved to the committee and how much delegated to the treasurer and his or her staff. In practice, decision about what is going to happen to interest rates over the next few months and also on the interpretation of internal forecasts are often taken by consensus between colleagues, and the forum of a treasury committee allows broad policy to be formed while the specialist dealers and other staff are able to make the more short term judgements. As with every other type of management, the proper selection of staff is critical to controls. The standard personnel procedures in selecting staff apply even more to treasury staff because of the level of financial risk involved. Financial controls are essential but these should not be regarded as complete in themselves. Once authorities are in place, deliberate breaches (such as a dealer exceeding authority) should lead to instant dismissal even if there was no intention to benefit personally. (Breaches are, of course, different from mistakes such as quoting a wrong account number, where additional training or better controls might be more appropriate.)

Membership of the treasury committee

It will be a matter of style and the size of the group as to whether or not this is a formal subcommittee of the board (rather like the audit committee). If it is a subcommittee, then it will probably be composed entirely of directors with the treasurer and possibly his or her deputy in attendance.

Often, a more practical forum is to bring together individuals who are conversant with the techniques and instruments involved, but who may not necessarily be involved in direct treasury management. In this case, the finance director and the financial controller together with the treasurer (plus deputy, probably) might be joined by other non-financial staff with a view to reaching balanced judgements. In particular, the assessment of risk may make someone like the company secretary a useful participant.

Agenda

A typical agenda might include the following.

Review of action since the last meeting

This could cover the actual outturn compared with expectations of decisions taken at previous meetings. There could also be a review of actual interest costs compared with given market indicators, such as average 3-month LIBOR.

Examination of cash flow forecasts

In addition to a balanced discussion of future funding or deposit arrangements, the committee can consider the sensitivities of the cash flow and may spot errors or risks that had been missed. This type of discussion allows a spreading of risk in terms of decision-making. It is unwise to rely entirely on the judgement of one individual.

Review of economic indicators

Perhaps quarterly, the committee should review the major economic forecasts for the economies in which the group operates. This might take the form of a summary of certain bank economist forecasts, giving a range of views on future interest rates and currency rates. The committee could then come to its own view on what might happen to rates. As discussed earlier, the company needs to come to its own view on rates before it can decide whether any hedging needs to take place.

As an alternative to a summary of bank forecasts, the company might employ a specific forecasting service which would create reports specifically for the company.

Short term interest rates

In practice, decisions about interest rates up to 6 months ahead may be delegated to operational staff, but the combination of the cash flow forecasts and the committee's views on future interest rates can provide some direction on whether to keep rates short or long and how much protection through the use of hedging instruments needs to be taken out.

Long term interest rates

If appropriate, the committee may take decisions (or make recommendations to the board) about the structure of long term interest rates.

Frequency

Meetings might be held monthly, or for less complex groups, perhaps quarterly. In the meantime it must be clear who is responsible for reviewing the position and how decisions can be taken between meetings. In practice, the treasurer (or appropriate subordinate for large groups) will review the detailed position on a weekly or daily basis.

Dealing and controls

In practice, much of the risk in treasury occurs through dealing. The appropriate policies described above should set out the limits for both individuals and counterparties. These limits are essential and where limits have been exceeded and controls not observed, large losses have arisen. These losses occur typically either because the company is using instruments that it does not understand or because controls are not complied with (including frequent spot checks).

171

Staff who deal should have no responsibility for processing accounting entries or for making settlements or reconciling (this is termed 'duality'). Thereafter, there should be spot checks carried out by an internal or external auditor to ensure compliance. These checks, however, do not remove the need for accurate and timely reporting.

The Association of Corporate Treasurers issued the following guidance note to its members in 1990 to assist them in their dealings with the financial markets. It is designed to illustrate the key control features that should be in place. It is not intended as a substitute for internal control manuals which should be specifically written and implemented within every treasury operation.

1 Treasury procedures should be designed so that any error can be readily identified and quickly resolved. It is generally recognised that in order to achieve this objective, it is necessary to have as much segregation of responsibilities as possible within treasury, subject to the number of staff involved, between the different functions, namely dealing, processing of deals ('back office'), settlement procedures and reconciliations.

2 All relationships with counterparties should be subject to a mandate. The mandate, while not a substitute for adequate internal controls, should set down appropriate constraints. With regard to dealing, the constraints to be covered should include:
   (a) naming the personnel authorised to deal and the limits of their dealing authority;
   (b) naming the personnel to whom deal confirmations must be sent – in no circumstances should a deal confirmation be sent to a dealer;

3 A dealing limit should be set for each counterparty and utilisation against the limit should be regularly monitored. Depending on the nature of transactions undertaken more than one limit may need to be set. A settlement limit will normally

be required. Others, such as forward limits, sometimes even split by forward time frame, may also be required.

4 Wherever possible, dealers should obtain at least two simultaneous quotations before entering into a deal. A deal should only be struck with a counterparty which has sufficient unutilised approved dealing limit.

5 Consideration, especially in larger corporate treasury operations, should be given to tape recording all telephone conversations undertaken from dealing and settlement clerk positions. Tapes should be retained until counterparties' confirmations have been received, checked and any discrepancies resolved.

6 In manual systems, the deal ticket is the prime record of each deal. It should be raised by the dealer immediately the deal is struck. The annotation of execution time on the deal ticket is prudent and can be an important audit trail. All deal tickets should be prenumbered and accounted for. They should be used as the control document for all further processing.

7 Where the dealing room is computerised, direct entry of deal information may eliminate the need to write a deal ticket. In these circumstances, because there would be no written evidence of the deal, tape recording becomes essential.

8 All deals must be logged in the organisation's records. Treasury positions should be readily identifiable and effectively controlled.

9 Once recorded, a letter of confirmation ('outgoing confirmation') should be produced for every deal. This confirmation must be produced by staff independent of the dealers. Each confirmation should be checked against the deal ticket (or other record) before the confirmation is authorised and issued. This is to ensure the counterparty is sent an accurate record of the deal. Once checked and agreed, the confirmation should be signed, preferably by two authorised signatories, before it is sent. Wherever practicable, an outgoing confirmation should be sent on the same day that the deal is struck.

10 In the same way that a deal confirmation is sent out, the counterparty should send a confirmation ('incoming confirmation'). The incoming confirmation is an important document. It enables the company to ensure that its record of a deal is accurate, that no problems will arise when the deal falls due for settlement and that no unauthorised transactions have been entered into.

11 Checking of incoming confirmations must never be undertaken by a dealer.

12 If there is a delay in receiving an incoming confirmation, the counterparty must be informed promptly. Settlement should only be made against a confirmed and matched deal.

13 Exceptional circumstances may arise, for example same-day value transactions, where it is not possible to exchange and match written confirmations before settlement. In such cases the level of other internal controls must be raised and other appropriate security arrangements put in place. Such arrangements may include recording of settlement instructions, secure fax confirmation or tested telex. Again, dealers must never be involved in this process and settlements must be made only if adequate alternative confirmation and matching procedures have been followed.

14 It is important that any confirmation difference is resolved as soon as possible. A formal discrepancy reporting procedure should be established so that discrepancy investigations are properly controlled.

Clearly, this level of detail may be difficult for sole traders or for small not-for-profit organisations. However, the spirit and principles apply to all organisations. The guidance note sets out the stages involved in a deal and in practice the use of dealing slips will ensure that the procedures are followed. Once a deal is struck, the dealer should always read back the details to avoid misunderstandings.

The stages involved in executing a deal are:

1 Use a preprinted, prenumbered dealing ticket. Fill in the parameters of the deal such as type of deal (e.g. deposit), why it is being undertaken, the time, which banks are quoting, the screen rate, etc.
2 Get further approvals if beyond dealer's authority.
3 Telephone a series of dealers and obtain quotes.
4 Choose the best quote and deal.
5 Double check details with counterparty.
6 Give settlement instructions (or agree to send them later).
7 Complete details on dealing ticket calculating interest or settlement amount.
8 Diarise the deal maturity or notice/action date, as appropriate.
9 Pass deal ticket to colleague for checking and position updating.
10 Pass details to colleague for funds movement instructions.

Derivatives

There has been considerable attention paid to derivatives over recent years because of losses made in a number of high profile cases in the US, the UK and elsewhere. These losses have, in the main, occurred because the organisation either did not realise it was speculating (such as writing options) or was not applying appropriate controls (e.g. Barings). Dealing in derivatives, if properly understood, should be no different from dealing in other instruments. In the UK, the Futures and Options Association (involving a large number of professional bodies) has published guidelines for end users of derivatives entitled 'Managing Derivatives Risk'. The main summary follows and is reproduced with their approval.

1 The board of directors (or its equivalent) should establish and approve an effective policy for the use of derivatives which is

175

consistent with the strategy, commercial objectives and risk appetite of the underlying business of the organisation, and should approve the instruments to be used and how they are to be used.

2 Senior management should establish clear written procedures for implementing the derivatives policy set by the board, covering such matters as dealing authority, reporting lines, risk limits, counterparty and documentation approvals and valuation procedures and should regularly review their operation and effectiveness.

3 Senior management should ensure that derivative activities are properly supervised and are subject to an effective framework of internal controls and audits to ensure that transactions are in compliance with both external regulations (including the capacity to enter into derivative transactions) and internal policy (including procedures for the execution, confirmation, recording and processing and settlement of transactions).

4 Senior management should establish a sound risk management function providing, wherever possible, for an independent framework for reporting, monitoring and controlling all aspects of risk, valuing exposures, assessing performance, imposing, monitoring and enforcing position and other limits, stress testing and contingency planning.

5 Procedures should be in place to provide for a full analysis of all credit risks to which the organisation will be exposed, the minimisation of such risks through the use of collateral or other credit enhancement techniques and the management of such risks through the use of credit limits for each counterparty covering the organisation's aggregate exposure to that counterparty.

6 Procedures should be in place for the monitoring and management of legal risk, covering issues of legal capacity and authority, compliance with relevant statutory requirements and the need for appropriate documentation dealing with the nature of the relationship between the parties, the terms of the transaction, netting provisions and, where relevant, credit enhancement arrangements.

176

Style of company

The precise way of operating will depend greatly upon the style and culture of the organisation. Many decentralised companies have very small central treasuries. The scope for managing liquidity will therefore depend upon how much responsibility is left with the operating units. Companies may decide that even decisions about risk should be left at the operating unit, otherwise the entrepreneurial spirit will be diminished. Banks, however, like to have a central point of contact. This may be the finance director in a small head office.

For companies with strong central financial controls and for small businesses, the precise method of operation will need to suit the particular company as that company, in the end, has its own cash cycle and, therefore, liquidity needs. Overall, the basic principles to follow are:

- have a clear policy and view of what you wish to achieve before dealing;
- understand the instruments and their risks before dealing;
- ensure that the policy has clearly set levels of acceptable loss;
- ensure each individual has clearly set authority;
- ensure clear segregation of duties between dealing and monitoring;
- have regular, timely and accurate management reports.

Glossary

Acceptance credit: a short term financing facility under which the borrower draws bills of exchange on a bank which accepts them and discounts them in the market to provide cash for the borrower.

Arbitrage: operating simultaneously in two different, but mutually relevant, markets so as to profit from a temporary misalignment between them.

At the money: used to describe an option where the strike price is the same as the underlying commodity.

Bank float: time spent by a remittance in the banking system during which its amount is available to neither the payer nor the payee.

Bank transfer: a remittance process whereby a payer makes a payment at any branch of any bank for the account of a payee at any branch of the same or other bank. Also called credit transfer or direct transfer.

Banker's payment: payment order issued by a bank on behalf of its customer, whereby the recipient looks to the bank for settlement, thus minimising credit risk. Also called a banker's draft.

Base rate: basic lending rate of a bank or financial institution in the UK. Used as the reference rate for overdraft lending.

Basic cover (Export Credits Guarantee Department (ECGD)): the basic credit insurance guarantee or policy, i.e. the comprehensive guarantee, the supplemental extended terms guarantee or the specific guarantee.

Basis: the price difference between a financial futures contract and its underlying contract.

Basis point: 1/100th of 1%, i.e. 0.01%.

Bid–offer spread: the difference between two rates at which a bank is willing to borrow and lend funds or to buy and sell a currency or other financial instrument: the difference represents its dealing margin.

Bill of exchange: an unconditional order in writing addressed by one person (the drawer) to another, signed by the person giving it, requiring the person to whom it is addressed to pay on demand, or at a fixed or determinable future time, a sum certain in money, to or to the order of, a specified person or to bearer.

Bond (security): an interest-bearing certificate of debt, usually for a term of 5 years or more, executed under seal.

Certificate of deposit (CD): evidence of a deposit with a specified bank or building society repayable on a fixed date. It is a negotiable instrument.

Cleared balance: balance on a bank account excluding any receipts which do not yet represent cleared value.

Cleared value: the time at which a credit to a customer's bank account becomes fully available to the customer, and effective for calculating interest and for establishing the undrawn balance of a facility (if overdrawn).

Clearing: the process by which a payment through the banking system is transferred from the payer's to the payee's account.

Clearing house: an organisation guaranteeing settlement of trades on a futures exchange.

Collection account: a bank account opened for the specific purpose of speeding up the receipt of cleared value for remittances from specific customers or groups of customers, usually at a distant or foreign location or in a foreign currency. In the USA called a 'lockbox'.

Commercial credit risk: the risk that a customer will not pay on time, due to its insolvency or other causes specific to the customer rather than to its country or currency.

Commercial paper: unsecured promissory notes, usually issued by companies.

Commitment fee: a percentage per annum charged by a lender on the daily balance of a borrowing facility, usually charged on the undrawn balance of the facility.

Confirmed irrevocable letter of credit (CILC): an irrevocable letter of credit not merely notified but also confirmed to the payee by a bank usually in its own country, which amounts to a guarantee of payment by that bank so long as the payee complies with the terms of the credit. (Note that if the bank is not in a creditworthy country, there may be foreign exchange control problems.)

Confiscation risk: the risk that assets in a foreign country may be confiscated, expropriated or nationalised, or that the distant owner's control may be interfered with.

Correspondent bank: a bank in one country which, when so required, acts as an agent for a bank in another country, typically formalised by the holding of reciprocal bank accounts.

Depth of market: an indication of the volume of interest by both buyers and sellers. The opposite of a 'thin market'.

Direct transfer: see bank transfer.

Duration: the average of the maturity of all of the cash flows of a security, measured by the present value of each cash flow. Used in the management of interest rate risk by comparing the duration of the assets and the liabilities of a portfolio of securities.

Eligible bills: acceptance credits drawn subject to the Bank of England's rules on eligibility and accepted by certain banks whose acceptances are eligible for rediscount at the finest rates at the Bank of England.

Euro-(banks, currency, deposit, dollar, sterling, bond): a Eurocurrency deposit is a deposit in a bank account located outside the banking regulations of the country which issues the currency. Thus a Eurodollar deposit is a US dollar deposit held outside the USA or in an international banking facility in the USA. The prefix 'Euro' is often synonymous with 'offshore'.

Factoring: buying invoiced debts, and taking responsibility from the seller for sales accounting and debt collection.

Financial futures: contracts for the delivery at a future date of specified financial instruments or currency deposits; such contracts, like commodity futures, are traded in formal, open-outcry markets.

Float: see bank float.

Floating rate note (FRN): bonds on which the rate of interest is established periodically by reference to short term interest rates.

Forfaiting: acceptance by a bank (forfaitor) of medium – or long term bills of exchange without recourse to the seller.

Forward forward: a contract with a bank for a term borrowing or deposit to commence at a stated future date but at a rate specified at the time of the contract.

Futures: contracts for the delivery at a future date of standard amounts of a commodity, or a financial instrument or of a currency; such contracts are traded in formal, open outcry markets.

Gilt-edged securities: British government stocks.

Hedge: to take action to protect the business against price fluctuations, usually in exchange or interest rates.

Irrevocable letter of credit: a letter of credit which cannot be cancelled by the payer or its bank which issued the letter of credit.

Inter-bank: any transaction between banks, including deposits by one bank with another in the inter-bank market at inter-bank bid and offer rates, i.e. the rates at which a bank is willing to accept or make such deposits respectively.

Interest rate exposure: the cost to the business of changes in interest rates.

Invoice discounting: a commercial creditor sells its invoices to a factor (see factoring) at a discount for immediate cash; invoice discounting does not include sales accounting and debt collecting. The creditor still has to collect the debt for the factor.

Issuing and paying agent: a bank or other party which holds the notes (e.g. commercial paper) on behalf of a borrower until required to be issued and which handles the payments on issue and maturity of the notes.

Letter of credit: a formal undertaking by an importer's bank at the importer's request and in accordance with the importer's instructions either to pay, negotiate or accept bills of exchange drawn by the exporter or to authorise another bank to do this, against specific documents, provided that the terms of the credit are complied with. Such a credit can be revocable or irrevocable.

LIBID: London inter-bank bid rate.

LIBOR: London inter-bank offered rate. The rate at which banks will lend funds to another prime bank.

Liquid (instrument): one which the purchaser is readily able to sell before maturity.

Long position: assets exceed liabilities in given commodity. The opposite of a short position.

Mandate: authority given to a bank to open an account, defining the way in which it is to be operated.

Margin: (a) difference between buying and selling price; (b) the change in value in a contract traded on a futures exchange which has to be matched with a cash deposit. Also the initial deposit made when purchasing the contract.

Maturity: the date at which a debt or other payments fall due.

Maturity gap analysis: a common method of measuring interest rate exposure.

Maturity structure: the pattern of maturities among the assets and liabilities of the business.

Modified duration: a measure of the interest rate sensitivity or the volatility of the price of an instrument for a given small change in yield.

Money-market: consists of financial institutions and dealers in money and credit; in the UK the Bank of England, the deposit banks and the discount and accepting houses.

Multiple option facility (MOF): a credit facility allowing the borrower to determine the borrowing instrument, interest rate period, amount and currency, without prejudicing the total amount available over an agreed term.

Negotiable instrument: any financial instrument like bills of exchange, promissory notes, cheques, banknotes, CDs, share warrants, or bearer shares or debentures, the title of which passes without notice to the person liable on the instrument and in which a transferee in good faith and for a consideration of value acquires an indefeasible title.

Option: the right, but not the obligation, to buy (call) or sell (put) a commodity.

Option, American: an option which may be exercised at any time prior to expiration.

Option, call: the right to buy a commodity.

Option, European: an option which may only be exercised on its expiration date.

Option, put: the right to sell a commodity.

Repo: see repurchase agreement.

Repurchase agreement: a sale to an investor of a security and a simultaneous agreement to buy it back at a predetermined date prior to maturity at an agreed rate. Used to finance holdings of securities and also as a form of secured investment.

Revolving limits: a limit of a borrowing facility which permits the re-borrowing of amounts repaid, and restricts the total outstanding balance.

Sales mix: the proportions of business sales with different operating characteristics like gross margins, so that a change in these proportions would change the overall performance of the business.

Secondary market: a market in financial instruments after their issue, which improves the liquidity of the holders of those instruments.

Short deposits: current accounts, overnight deposits and money at call; deposits with longer maturities are term deposits.

Spread: see bid–offer spread.

Stop loss: an order to sell a financial instrument when its price falls to a specified level.

Tender panel: a group of banks tendering competitively to lend money.

Tender panel agent: co-ordinates tender panel bids and interfaces with the borrower.

Tenor = usance: the period for which a bill of exchange or promissory note is expressed to run to maturity; a tenor bill contrasts with a sight bill which is payable on sight.

Term deposit, time deposit: deposits, including CDs, for periods longer than sight deposits.

Thin market: see depth of market.

Value, value date: the point in time when a bank remittance actually becomes available to the payee for use.

Appendix
Useful calculations

Note: where x is the rate to be converted and y is the revised rate.

To semi-annualize an annual rate x

$$y = \left(\sqrt{\frac{x}{100} + 1} \right) - 1 \times 200$$

To make an annual rate x into quarterly rate y

$$y = \left(\sqrt[4]{\frac{x}{100} + 1} \right) - 1 \times 400$$

To annualize a semi-annual rate x

$$y = \left(\frac{x}{200} + 1 \right)^2 - 1 \times 100$$

To annualize a quarterly rate x

$$y = \left(\frac{x}{400} + 1\right)^4 - 1 \times 100$$

To semiannualize a quarterly rate x

$$y = \left(\frac{x}{400} + 1\right)^2 - 1 \times 200$$

True yield basis of y from a given discount rate x

For a 365-day year basis and for a discount period of d days

$$y = \frac{36\,500x}{36\,500 - xd}$$

To convert different yield bases

Where: MMY is money-market yield; BEY is bond equivalent yield; ISMA is ISMA yield; D is discount

$$\text{BEY} = \text{MMY} \times \frac{365}{360}$$

$$\text{MMY} = \text{BEY} \times \frac{360}{365}$$

$$\text{D} = y\left(\frac{1}{1 + \left[\frac{y}{100} \times \frac{\text{days}}{\text{basis}}\right]}\right)$$

(where basis is either 360 or 365 and y is MMY or BEY)

$$BEY = n \times \left\{ (1 + ISMA)^{\frac{1}{n}} - 1 \right\} \times 100$$

(where n is the number of compounding periods)

$$ISMA = \left(\left\{ 1 + \frac{BEY}{n} \right\}^{n} - 1 \right) \times 100$$

Further reading

Corporate cash management: strategy and practice, Philippa Foster Back (Woodhead Publishing Ltd)

Principles of corporate finance, Richard Brealey and Stuart Myers (McGraw-Hill)

The sterling commercial paper market, Charles Mitchell (Woodhead-Faulkner)

Financial risk and internal control, ed. John Grout (ACT)

The London Code of Conduct (Bank of England)

A handbook of financial mathematics, Peter Cartledge (Euromoney)

Derivatives for directors, Richard Cookson (ACT)

The financial jungle, Phil Rivett and Peter Speak (Coopers & Lybrand)

Options, futures and other derivative securities, John Hull (Prentice Hall)

Financial risk management, Brian Eales (McGraw-Hill)

Electronic banking and security, Brian Welch (Woodhead Publishing Ltd)

Index